The
Drama Free
Workbook

The
Drama Free
Workbook

*practical exercises for managing
unhealthy family relationships*

• • • • •

NEDRA GLOVER TAWWAB

A TarcherPerigee Book

tarcherperigee

an imprint of Penguin Random House LLC
penguinrandomhouse.com

Copyright © 2024 Nedra Glover Tawwab
Penguin Random House supports copyright. Copyright fuels creativity, encourages diverse voices, promotes free speech, and creates a vibrant culture. Thank you for buying an authorized edition of this book and for complying with copyright laws by not reproducing, scanning, or distributing any part of it in any form without permission. You are supporting writers and allowing Penguin Random House to continue to publish books for every reader.

TarcherPerigee with tp colophon is a registered trademark of Penguin Random House LLC

Most TarcherPerigee books are available at special quantity discounts for bulk purchase for sales promotions, premiums, fundraising, and educational needs. Special books or book excerpts also can be created to fit specific needs. For details, write SpecialMarkets@penguinrandomhouse.com.

ISBN 9780593712672

Printed in the United States of America
1st Printing

Book design by Shannon Nicole Plunkett

Contents

Author's Note

Our family of origin is the most impactful relationship structure in our lives. For better or worse, or somewhere in between, the family dynamics we grew up with affect how we experience relationships—everything from how we attach to others to how we explore new relationships, and even how we think about ourselves. Becoming an adult does not mean an automatic fresh start. Changing these patterns requires intention, courage, and the willingness to sacrifice the short-term comfort that comes with maintaining the status quo. Even when we decide we're ready to break free from old family patterns, we often discover how deeply ingrained they are within us.

Drama takes many forms in families, from sibling conflict to parenting our parents. Judging one problem as worse or bigger than another is subjective. Only you can decide which issues you can live with and which relationships you'll need to manage differently going forward.

Take good care of yourself as you read this workbook. Family issues can cause old wounds to resurface and bring new problems to light that you didn't know needed to be addressed. Be aware that avoiding your feelings about the hard stuff won't help your progression. Feel everything that comes up, because it's rising to the top for a reason. Change isn't easy, yet it's the only way to get to the version of yourself that feels best.

Taking the First Step

People often avoid thinking about the difficult relationships in their lives. Somehow, the belief is "If I stop thinking about it, I will feel better." That's partially true, but it's a short-term solution. The reality is, if you feel it, process it, and allow the thoughts to come up, that will also help you feel better and is a long-term, lasting solution. Avoidance via substances, mindless scrolling, working obsessively hard to be successful, or moving far away won't change what is deeply embedded in your brain and behaviors.

Far too often, people who appear outwardly successful—by means of degrees, a great job, or fame—still suffer within, despite how much they seem to "have it all together." Success can be an avoidance strategy. Conversely, many people are outwardly in the throes of dealing with family trauma. The best thing we can do for ourselves is to face what we were taught to avoid or not share.

When I was kid, I saw relatives drowning in other people's problems or victimized by people who hadn't changed and were in denial about their own issues (but were clear about everyone else's issues, of course). As I got older, I discovered that it's possible to change, and that doing so creates a ripple effect in both comfortable and not-so-comfortable ways. For instance, when we decide not to engage in certain behaviors, it separates us from others, and it can feel lonely to be without these family members. Nevertheless, noticing that something is wrong and deciding to do something about it is brave and life-changing.

My first book cultivated the idea that we need more practice building healthy boundaries in family relationships. The rules of engagement apply to family and can be shifted to foster the relationships that matter most to us. Within families, the practice of boundaries can be unique and is often cumbersome. This workbook will help you break down barriers and create lasting changes.

When you let go of family patterns and create your own life, you design your relationships to reflect the life you want. As you do this, some people in your life will change (to the degree they can), and others will stay the same. It helps to accept people as they are, but it isn't a solution to particularly troubling relationships. Your greatest power lies in changing yourself and aligning with your own values.

IN THIS BOOK, YOU'LL LEARN AND PRACTICE HOW TO

- Define who you are and what you want to carry over from what you learned in your family

- Confront what drama in your family looked like in the past and how it feels now

- Create a unique road map for how to manage or release complex relationships

- Identify how certain family practices in the past laid the groundwork for the unhealthy dynamics you experience today

- Grow in your relationship with yourself as a method for improving your relationship with others

HOW TO USE THIS BOOK

Move slowly through these pages. Be like a turtle—deliberate and at ease. What has taken years to create can't be undone in one week.

When new clients enter therapy, they routinely ask, "How long will I need to come?" We try to get through some of the most challenging moments in our lives quickly, but I encourage you to take some time with yourself and with family. Many things in this book will have to be practiced over and over. I have revisited many of my favorite books—*The Autobiography of Malcolm X*, *She's Come Undone*, *Sisters of the Yam*, and *What I Know For Sure*—many times. Every time I go back to them, I discover something new. I'm constantly shifting, so what I pull out of them changes based on my development. Use this book over and over to be met where you are and to refine your tools.

Reading my book *Drama Free: A Guide to Managing Unhealthy Family Relationships* will be helpful. However, this book is a stand-alone resource and a hands-on tool for exploring these concepts and applying them in your own life.

Pause and Return

Notice your response to the reading material. Take a break from it when you notice shifts in your behavior, such as irritability, difficulty concentrating, sleep issues, or fixation. Return once your intense feelings have subsided. The workbook is intended to help, not to cause further harm. Thinking about the workbook is okay, but not being able to resume life can be a sign to find some support while reading the material.

Therapy can be used as a supplemental tool to help you with the difficult areas you're trying to resolve. Having a space to process what happened while exploring difficult changes can be just what you need to foster new practices.

Lists

Lists are a way to express more than one thought about something. You can feel many things at once or have several thoughts about a topic. Therefore, in the chapters that follow, I will prompt you to create lists of ideas. Family is complicated, and giving yourself space to explore possibilities is essential.

Journaling

Throughout this workbook, you'll find questions and prompts to help you write through your feelings. There's something magical about honestly allowing yourself to answer questions. The focus of journaling is *releasing*. Get thoughts and feelings out of your head, on paper, in your notes app, or on a voice note. Holding memories, conversations, and emotions in has not helped you. Use journaling as a tool to process the practice of changing. Here are a few questions to consider as you journal:

1. How does it feel to reevaluate my perspective?

2. As I'm working through the book, what concerns do I have about implementing new practices?

3. What memories were prompted while reading?

Keep your journal private if you are not ready to share your thoughts.

Checklists

Certain concepts, such as emotional neglect or abuse, can be hard to understand and recognize, and a checklist can help you know if you meet specific criteria. Checklists are a way to discover what you might need to address and what you might see in others. You will notice that some lists don't exactly fit your situation, but take a look at them anyway. Use them as a general guide, not as a definitive diagnostic tool.

. . . .

I will share exercises throughout the book to help you grow your knowledge base and apply key concepts. Remember that no one is checking your work, so be very honest with yourself. Before completing an exercise, close your eyes and take two or three deep breaths (in through your nose and out through your mouth).

This workbook will call on you to release some of the difficult thoughts and beliefs you've been carrying about yourself and others. There will be times when you feel the need to step away. Do so, but remember to return. Don't quit. You can move at your own pace and pause as needed.

Some of us have not one but many issues in our family. Use the space below to identify your three most significant challenges with family.

1._____

_____

_____

_____

2._____

_____

_____

_____

3. _____

_____

_____

_____

Remember that neither you nor Rome was built in a day. This is a process of slow uncovering, rebuilding, and renaissance.

CHAPTER 1

Uncovering
What Happened
to You

*Where you grew up, who you grew up with, and the things
you experienced in your home will have lifelong
implications for who you become.*

According to the *Oxford English Dictionary*, "dysfunctional" refers to something that doesn't operate properly. There are many definitions of "family," but the one I like best is "two or more people related by blood, adoption, commitment, or familial ties." When we put both definitions together, we have "two or more people in a relationship that isn't functioning in a healthy way."

For example, Lydia was talking to her mother, Martha, and casually mentioned being from a "dysfunctional family." Immediately, Martha chimed in and said, "I'm not from a dysfunctional family, and neither are you." So it began. Lydia and Martha disagreed on what "dysfunctional" means. Some people may describe dysfunction as having patterns of abuse or substance misuse. In contrast, others may say a family is dysfunctional when you don't have a relationship in which you feel accepted by your parents or when you have a contentious relationship with a sibling. Everyone's right. Dysfunction is in the eye of the beholder. The label is essentially a way of saying "In my relationship with _____, I experienced _____." Your relationships may not mirror another family member's relationships, so there's not necessarily a need to agree on terms. Conversely, we shouldn't overuse the term to apply to every relationship mishap. It's a term best used for chronic, consistent, and impactful patterns.

The people who harmed you may not validate your experiences within the family. What you see as harmful can be what others accept as routine behavior or what they "have to deal with" from their family. The beautiful and freeing thing about being an adult is that you can curate the life you want.

Dysfunction isn't always black-and-white. What are some themes within your family that you would note as dysfunctional?

Here are a few examples to get you started:

> "In my family, my parents pushed getting good grades and participation in extracurricular activities. I wasn't able to relax and do many things that weren't educational. Now I struggle with feeling like I constantly need to be productive."

Dysfunction is in the eye of the beholder.

> "My mother was often on the go, partying with her friends. My siblings and I spent more time with caring family members and neighbors than with our mother. Now we don't have a close relationship with her, and she wonders why."

Describe a few of your own:

•
_____

_____

_____

•
_____

_____

•
_____

_____

_____

WE CAN ALL AGREE ON THIS—OR CAN WE?

Behaviors such as physical or sexual abuse and neglect are harmful behaviors. However, some people try to minimize the extent of abuse or neglect by focusing on the severity of the behaviors. What matters is the *impact*. A harmful act toward a child, for example, can have a profound impact on that child, while the adult might dismiss it—both in the moment and years later—as a brief second with no lasting effects, saying things like "It could have been worse."

For example, Bianca told her mother that a cousin had assaulted her. Her mother asked, "Was it penetration?" Since it wasn't, Bianca's assault was minimized, and she was told to stay away from her cousin at family gatherings. Many years later, she feels very anxious about attending a family gathering and harnesses resentment toward her mother for glossing over the incident.

ASSESSMENT: IDENTIFYING FAMILY DYSFUNCTION

Respond to the questions below by selecting "Yes" or "No." Remember that we aren't focused on severity; the event itself is enough. It's never our job to determine severity. We must focus on what happened, the impact, and what to do going forward.

1. Are secrets a part of your family culture (e.g., "What happens in our house stays in our house")? Yes No

2. Did you experience abuse or neglect in your home? Yes No

3. Did your parents often fight verbally or physically? Yes No

4. Did one or both of your caretakers misuse drugs or alcohol?
   Yes No

5. Do you have a contentious relationship with one or more of your siblings? Yes No

6. At family gatherings, is there often drama? Yes No

7. Do you feel disconnected from and misunderstood by your family?
   Yes No

8. Are poor behaviors that harm others enabled in your family?
   Yes No

9. When you express boundaries, are they respected? Yes No

10. Do your parents accept you for who you are? Yes No

Early in my career, I worked as a therapist for families involved with Child Protective Services in the greater Detroit area. Parents often didn't think the physical abuse was damaging enough to warrant their child being removed, but the State of Michigan disagreed. For health-care providers, mental health professionals, and teachers, we don't investigate; we report and respond. Clients know that some things will be reported if they inform a therapist, mainly abuse of a child (either young in age or older) or harm to themselves or another person. It's never easy letting someone know "I have to report this." However, it's done as a protection to those involved. In good conscience, I cannot minimize or ignore abuse.

Abuse, neglect, homelessness, substance abuse in the home, domestic violence, or having an incarcerated parent are all components that contribute to dysfunction within a family. What are some other things that you deem as clearly dysfunctional?

Everyone should agree that these are dysfunctional:

_____

_____

_____

_____

_____

_____

_____

In my family, we disagree about this being dysfunctional:

_____

_____

_____

_____

_____

_____

ENVIRONMENT MATTERS

Gardening is dear to my heart. Whether it's outdoors growing vegetables and flowers or indoors growing houseplants, the environment determines success. The soil (foundation), sunlight (exposure), and watering practices (nurturing) are key to any garden—vegetables, plants, or humans. You can't thrive without having certain conditions in place, so your home environment sustains you or sets you up for the challenges ahead. When a therapist asks, "Where did you first experience this?" it's because we know that many things sprout from where each of us started.

Things You May Pick Up from Your Environment

- Money management skills
- Communication skills
- Attachment style
- Values

- Patterns of substance use
- How you treat your children
- How you handle your mental health

How far back does your memory go? Let's explore some of the scenes you saw in your home in your earliest memories. Write down anything that comes to mind, whether positive, negative, or neutral.

I remember this about my environment growing up:

_____

_____

I remember this about my environment growing up:

_____

_____

I remember this about my environment growing up:

_____

_____

I remember this about my environment growing up:

_____

_____

I remember this about my environment growing up:

_____

_____

Are there any challenging memories that you find hard to write down? If so, what are they?

_____

_____

_____

_____

RUSHING TO RESILIENCE

There is a massive emphasis on resiliency in our culture. We give people very little time to sit in their stories before we rush along to the lesson or insist that they recognize the strength gained from their experiences. This aggressive, "brighter side" thinking takes away from what we feel. Let's stop "getting over it" and start *feeling it*.

> Let's stop
> "getting over it"
> and start
> feeling it.

Ultimately, our goal is healing and growth, but there are times when we need to just be upset or sad about what we went through. These experiences can actually make us better people—once we learn how to understand and process them. I wouldn't have been able to write *Set Boundaries, Find Peace* if not for a bit of trauma, but I also needed time to sit with what I went through.

"Sitting inside" our stories is different from being stuck inside them. When we're stuck, our emotions don't progress. When we're stuck, the telling of the story stays the same, the emotions don't evolve, and the frequency with which we tell the story remains the same. That doesn't mean that sharing our stories serves no purpose. Sometimes when we're telling a story repeatedly, we're seeking some connection or validation. This can be part of the process of growth—but pay attention to what you're looking for, and why.

When I work with clients who have phobias, I ask them to close their eyes and talk about what they're afraid of. I have them do this over and over. I do this with the intention that they repeat their story until their emotion changes. My hope is that this process will desensitize them. I'm not saying they shouldn't have any emotion, but I'm trying to help them decrease the intensity. When we rush ourselves through our stories, we reshape the stories themselves. We skip over how something made us feel to get to the part where we get over it. We force ourselves to be resilient even when we're not.

Have you ever felt pressured to be resilient? Where did that pressure come from?

_____

_____

_____

_____

Give yourself space to feel the things you're still processing. List some things you still need to finish.

Examples: My father didn't attend my graduation; my cousins bullied me; my grandmother was nicer to my aunt's children.

_____

_____

_____

_____

_____

_____

_____

_____

_____

Later in the workbook, we'll explore strategies to help you process your experiences. For now, focus on feeling. People show up to therapy with stories that have been pushed down deep inside because they've been trying to power through their challenging human moments without sitting long enough in their stories.

REPEAT AFTER ME

"I powered through hard times, and now I'm allowing myself to feel things."

"Things were hard, and I did what I needed to at the time."

"Resilience has allowed me to keep going. I'm offering myself an opportunity to explore what I couldn't then."

"I didn't have the tools and resources to be present."

"Being present wasn't an option."

RECLAIMING YOUR VOICE

Much of what you may have lost is the ability to talk about what hurts, what you missed, and how you feel. The most important person to be honest with, however, is yourself. You have to own your story and explore your narrative.

There was probably a time when your thoughts were more clear. Over the years, you may have learned to water them down. It's understandable that we speak carefully when we fear ruffling feathers, getting into trouble, or being isolated for what we speak up about.

People often use softer language to describe challenging moments, such as "he drank a lot" instead of "he was an alcoholic." When you are still processing what happened, saying it plainly can be difficult.

What do you say versus what really happened? As you describe the specific events you experienced, be honest about what occurred.

What You Say

Example: My grandfather yelled a lot at my grandmother and his children.

_____

_____

What Really Happened

Example: My grandfather was verbally abusive.

_____

_____

What You Say

_____

_____

What Really Happened

_____

_____

What You Say

_____

_____

What Really Happened

_____

_____

When you change the wording, notice what it feels like to shift that slight detail. The difference is in the details. Protecting others can be so unconsciously familiar that you do it intuitively without thinking about the impact on you.

What do you gain from remaining silent? You wouldn't do it if there wasn't a reason. Family issues are commonly protected for the following reasons:

- What happened in your family reflects your identity and your beliefs.

- It's embarrassing to share certain details of what happened, especially when the other person hasn't experienced anything similar to what you describe.

- Ignoring the problem keeps you in the good graces of others. When you acknowledge true events, you may be seen as a traitor.

In the podcast series *We Were Three*, author Rachel McKibbens describes how she became distant from her father and brother, who both later tragically died. She revisits many childhood moments when her father, an alcoholic, physically abused both her and her brother. During an acceptance speech for a high school acting award, McKibbens revealed that acting came easily for her because she had been "acting" for seventeen years. Her father called her a traitor for exposing the family secrets, and her brother remained silent.

What do you gain from remaining silent?

Sharing what really happened can cause issues within a dysfunctional system because the dysfunction is sustained on secrecy. You might not want to share it because you:

Fear that you're alone in your struggles and that no one else will understand. Believing that no one will understand is a heavy assumption. Books, support groups, and online communities exist to provide support for many of the issues you face. Communities are built of people who will uniquely understand what you're going through.

Fear judgment. Indeed, when people are ignorant about the differences of others, they can be mean or misinformed. Conversely, if more people were open, would they be less judgmental? Generally speaking, openness begets understanding.

Family secrets are a way to perpetuate unhealthy loyalty and unhealthy behaviors. If you are encouraged to keep certain relationship practices a secret, something out of sorts is likely happening. If you believed "What happens in this house stays in this house," you may feel ashamed about what happened. But vulnerability disconnects you from shame. Remember: Secrets perpetuate shame and delay healing.

Vulnerability disconnects you from shame.

KEEP HOPE ALIVE, BUT STAY ROOTED IN REALITY

Change happens suddenly, or it can take a long time to get there. Focus on your path and encourage others. But don't be detoured by others' lack of progress. Also, beating yourself up for all the years you wasted isn't a fair use of your time. Reclaim today! Move forward knowing that what happened can't be changed but that what will happen in the future is still unfolding.

You're ready now. I know this because you're reading this book. What made you ready to change?

_____

_____

_____

_____

_____

_____

_____

_____

It's a Process

Who told us that there is an end point to healing? Old wounds have scars; in third grade, I was accidentally stabbed in the arm with a pencil. The scar remains. It's smoothed over and smaller, yet still there. And I remember what happened.

Emotional, verbal, mental, and physical scars remain with us. When you let yourself experience them, you can move on faster, and you can breathe easier when you talk about them. Healing doesn't erase them, but it reduces their intensity.

What feels fresh, and what are you in the process of working through? List a few things below.

Unhealed

Example: I still come undone when I think about being spanked so severely that I had welts from the belt.

_____

_____

_____

_____

In the Process of Healing

Example: I no longer hear my mother's voice saying, "You have your dad's nose; it's big like his," when I look in the mirror.

_____

_____

_____

_____

Unhealed

_____

_____

_____

_____

In the Process of Healing

_____

_____

_____

_____

Unhealed

_____

_____

_____

_____

In the Process of Healing

_____

_____

_____

_____

UNHEALED TRAUMA IMPACTS HOW YOU SHOW UP IN YOUR RELATIONSHIPS

Maria, age thirty-two, was been able to date anyone seriously other than her high school sweetheart. When people started to commit, she became hesitant and pushed them away. Closeness felt awkward, since she dealt with so much in her life on her own. Even with friends, she found it hard to keep in touch, ask for help, or invite people to be there for her. She often referred to this as maintaining a healthy distance from others. Unfortunately, she practiced distancing in both healthy and unhealthy relationships. Staying away from relationships feels safe, but it's avoidance.

Have you practiced any of the following?

- Anxiety about committing to relationships

- Fear that others will harm you even when things are going well

- Constantly needing reassurance from another person

- Feelings of not being good enough

- Challenges communicating your needs

- Difficulty accepting positive feedback or help

Romantic relationships and friendships are often challenging when your foundational relationships aren't healthy.

Common thoughts that might circle as you try to venture into other relationships include the following:

"How can I trust my partner when I can't even trust my mother?"

"What if it happens again?"

"If my family doesn't love me, how can I expect anybody else to love me?"

"If my family would hurt me like that, anybody would."

Avoidance gets in the way of healing. *You have to be open to allowing people to be better to you than what you experienced.*

When you're from a dysfunctional family, love is defined as loyalty, even when you're harmed. They expect unlimited forgiveness, weak boundaries, and for you to quickly move past harm caused by others. Love does not include tolerating mistreatment. Love is caring, kind, respectful, and safe. Other definitions are used to brainwash you and keep you in unhealthy relationships. Abuse is not loving. Harm is not loving. But somehow, it's attached to love in dysfunctional families.

Avoidance gets in the way of healing.

As early as in middle school, my friends and I were honest about what was happening in our homes, and that honesty is what got me through many difficult moments. In the space below, share an example of an earlier time in your life when you were honest with someone about your experiences in your family:

_____

_____

_____

_____

_____

_____

_____

_____

_____

_____

As I've said, we move through the hard stuff by feeling it, and feeling isn't always the easiest thing to do. We want the opposite of feeling it. Clients sometimes ask, "How do I stop this feeling?" But that isn't what will help us heal.

Later in this workbook, we'll talk more about the importance of allowing yourself to feel and even go back and feel what you had to rush through.

In this chapter, what has been the most challenging thing for you to reflect on? What caused you to pause? Do you know why?

CHAPTER 2

The Big Three: Boundary Violations, Codependency, and Enmeshment

In dysfunctional family systems,
healthy boundaries are a threat to the status quo.

Boundaries are standards you have for yourself in your relationships with others. They are clear markers of what's acceptable and what's not acceptable. In unhealthy family systems, boundaries are often either too porous or too rigid. They don't provide the safety and clarity that healthy boundaries do and instead serve as a way to keep the unhealthy system alive.

Porous boundaries are too weak and let one person walk all over another. Rigid boundaries are too strong and keep people isolated and disconnected from each other.

A QUICK LESSON ON BOUNDARIES

Healthy boundaries vary from situation to situation and from person to person. In most cases, they should not be applied black-and-white, such as "I never want to help you with anything." Hopefully, they maintain a reasonable standard of expectations while allowing for some exceptions.

Over time, healthy boundaries can help children. A good example of this is in child-rearing. Young children need earlier bedtimes. Then, as they grow in age, they can stay up later. Without any guidelines (porous boundaries), kids won't get the sleep they need in order to function and grow in a healthy way. Conversely, if the bedtime guidelines are too strict (rigid), they don't account for special occasions, minor mishaps, and a forgiving "margin of error" that reflects the fact that life isn't perfect.

Healthy boundaries must be expressed both verbally (what we say) and behaviorally (what we do), and it's best when they're aligned in both of these ways. But rarely is that the case. We don't usually say, "Here's my boundary." As a result, we're often unclear, failing to state what we want, or we say things like "If your brother needs your help, you should always help him." You may even witness your parents always helping your siblings even when it's harmful or when they aren't equipped to help.

As children, we learn from our adult caregivers about how to form relationships with others. If our caregivers allow others to cross their boundaries, we may think it's normal. But just because it's normal doesn't mean it's healthy or right. It's important to set boundaries and not let anyone, even family, take advantage of us.

Hattie's mother, Anna, always told her to be careful about letting people use her, especially her friends. Whenever Hattie purchased a gift for a friend, Anna cautioned her, "Did they buy you a gift for your birthday?" or "I think that's too much for a friend." Anna demonstrated weak boundaries with family members and was told to "always," without exception, look out for her family. Hattie witnessed her mother in many family situations, such as disputes with siblings over money, having relatives live with them, and loaning things that were never returned. Hattie never experienced being taken advantage of by friends, even though she was trained to be suspicious of them. She understood that her mother was cautioning her to have healthy boundaries with friends, but not with family members.

Adult caregivers choose the relationships their children are in. In this way, they model how they exist in relationships. When adults allow others to violate their boundaries, children can interpret it as normal. So what's considered "normal" isn't always healthy, and it doesn't feel good to be taken advantage of by anyone, especially family.

How did your family model boundaries (or a lack of them)?
Example: My mom would threaten to stop lending my aunt money but always lent it to her in the end, despite knowing that my aunt wouldn't pay her back. Therefore, I thought it was normal to set a boundary but never actually enforce it.

_____

_____

_____

_____

_____

For dysfunctional systems to continue to operate, everyone has to remain in step with the unhealthy boundaries and ignorant of what would be healthy. When customary rules are challenged, the unhealthy system begins to break down.

In order to remain healthy in our relationships, personal autonomy is key. This involves having our own ideas, behaviors, and desires, regardless of those held in the system. In dysfunctional family relationships, however, autonomy can be seen as a threat.

Boundaries are for yourself and for your children (if you're a parent) in relationships with other family members, but they aren't a way to control people. They are more about what you will or won't do, as opposed to what you feel you "should" do in your relationships and your own life.

It's okay if your boundaries are not just like everyone else's. They're personal, and your mother's boundaries for child-rearing, for example, might not meet your expectations for today's parenting standards.

A QUICK LESSON ON CODEPENDENCY

Codependency is an unhealthy entanglement with the lives and emotions of others. If you're in a one-sided relationship with someone in which you consistently sacrifice your time, money, or well-being for them because you feel they'd be lost without you, that relationship is likely codependent. In relationships, notice when doing something for others harms your own quality of life. The goal is to care for people in a way that's healthy for both the other person and yourself. Being consumed with the lives of others is unhealthy, while not caring about anyone else at all would mean total detachment. The goal is to find a healthy balance between these two extremes.

In codependent relationships, the person who gives will receive only through being needed, not by having their needs met by the other person. Codependents lament, "I'm always there for other people, but when I need something, no one is there for me." This routinely happens when there is little reciprocity in a relationship.

Affirmations for Harmonious Caregiving

I can be there for you and also be present with myself.

I'm aware of my capacity.

I care for others, and I care for myself.

I have limits.

I give from a place of desire, not obligation.

Is Your Help Beneficial?

Kindness is an essential part of being in a relationship with someone. However, there are times when your kindness isn't actually helpful—and can even get in the way of someone else's growth (as well as your own). Below, describe a time when you helped someone and their situation improved. Then describe a time when you attempted to help someone and noticed that the situation was a recurring issue for the person, and your assistance didn't serve either of you well.

My Help Was Helpful

_____

_____

_____

_____

My Help Wasn't Very Helpful

_____

_____

_____

_____

Consider other situations like these, and respond below.

My Help Was Helpful

_____

_____

_____

_____

My Help Wasn't Very Helpful

_____

_____

_____

_____

_____

My Help Was Helpful

_____

_____

_____

_____

My Help Wasn't Very Helpful

_____

_____

_____

_____

Perhaps you aren't the person in your family with a codependent relationship. But witnessing two or more other people in an unbalanced relationship can be tough to watch, and can even create feelings of isolation. I have helped clients come to terms with being outsiders in their family dynamic. Groups within groups often exist—such as father and son, or mother and daughter—and all types of bonds can leave others out of the system.

For example, Iris watched her mother financially support her older sister, Emily, while also helping to care for Emily's children. Iris didn't receive the same level of support from their mother. It impacted her relationship with Emily because even though Emily knew it was unfair, she still accepted the help from their mother. Iris watched as their mom spent holidays and weekends with her sister and wouldn't attend Iris's events unless Emily could also come.

What codependent relationships have you observed in your family?

_____

_____

_____

_____

How do codependent bonds in your family affect your relationships with the people involved?

_____

_____

_____

_____

One-Sided Relationships

In some cases, it makes sense for a relationship to be one-sided, like the relationship between a parent and young child. Kids aren't in a position to treat adults the same way we treat them. But for healthy adult relationships, there's generally an understanding that there will be reciprocity, with give-and-take from both parties. This doesn't mean the reciprocity will show up in exactly the same way, however. If you help someone with a home project, for example, it doesn't mean they must help you with your next home project. They might support you emotionally by cheering you on during a difficult time at work, for example.

When a relationship is one-sided without a healthy give-and-take, it's only a problem when one person begins to feel challenged by it. If you want to change the dynamic of such a relationship, try the following strategies:

- State the issue. For example, "It seems like whenever we connect, I always invite you to do something. I would like for you to initiate some of our interactions." Let the person know what you're missing. When you state the issue, you also express your needs and open up a conversation about whether the other person can meet them.

- Dial back on initiating. Sometimes, we say another person demands a lot of our time and attention when it's actually us who initiates most, if not all, of the interactions. Do you constantly call them? Do you frequently invite them to come over or go out? If this makes you feel resentful, you can decide to initiate less often.

- Don't be afraid to repeat yourself. If you stated your needs a couple of weeks ago, and it feels like nothing has changed, it's okay to remind the person of what you discussed.

- Accept that the other person may not change. Some people are interested in participating in relationships in a different way than we'd prefer. Some people will only step up in certain ways. If you're in that situation, you may not need to end the relationship, though that's certainly an option. Another choice is to change the way you interact with that person. Think about what you might want to shift in order to remain in a relationship with them. For example, you may decide to hang out with them only when you truly want to do so.

Using the diagram below, evaluate your relationships with key people. Take time to think about who should be where. Be honest. Write what feels natural to you, not what you think you "should" say.

Relationships that require a lot of emotional energy with low give and lots of take

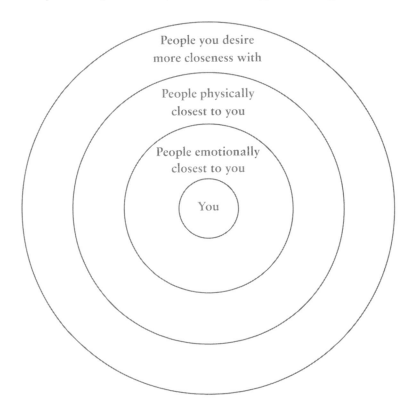

People you desire
more closeness with

People physically
closest to you

People emotionally
closest to you

You

Consider this:

What was your measure of closeness?

Were you surprised where you placed some people?

Did you leave anyone out? If so, who and why?

A QUICK LESSON ON ENMESHMENT

Families are their own cultural entities, and as I've said, there's an ecosystem within each family as to what's considered appropriate and inappropriate. In dysfunctional families, everyone is usually expected to think, believe, feel, and act similarly. This is called "enmeshment," in which there is no separation between the thoughts, beliefs, feelings, and actions of others and your own.

Our differences, however, are what make us unique. When we're unable to be unique in our relationships with others, it means we have to hide parts of ourselves to feel accepted. In an enmeshed family, our differences threaten the ecosystem.

For example, Morgan's parents and two sisters were all married, but Morgan was happily single at age twenty-nine. Her family often challenged her beliefs about marriage and her comfort with being single. While she wasn't against marriage, she wasn't in a hurry and was also open to a lifetime partnership that didn't involve marriage at all. Her beliefs were often the topic at family gatherings.

Arguments and estrangements can occur over our differences. In your family, what beliefs do you share, and what beliefs are dissimilar? Check the appropriate columns on the next page.

	SIMILAR	DIFFERENT
Religion		
Political views		
Relationship expectations		
Family planning		
Child-rearing		
Food choices		
Views on body/appearance		
Other:		
Other:		

"UNBECOMING"—MOVING AWAY
FROM ENMESHMENT

Healthy aspects of becoming an adult include differentiation (becoming more of your true self) and also unlearning what isn't working for you in your relationships and in your life. With clients, I've seen this differentiation process happen anywhere from childhood to older adulthood. Coming into yourself can be a long process for those from families in which it's only considered okay to be just like everyone else. Moments in life that accelerate differentiation include intermingling more with your peer group, leaving home, committing to a serious romantic relationship, moving far away from family, or just becoming tired of the status quo.

No two people are completely alike, even from the same family.

What do you share in common with your family members?

_____

_____

_____

_____

_____

In what ways are you different from them?

_____

_____

_____

_____

_____

Are these differences judged as good or bad?

_____

_____

_____

_____

What differences do _you_ judge as good or bad?

_____

_____

_____

_____

On an episode of the TV show *Abbott Elementary*, a teacher named Barbara (played by Sheryl Lee Ralph) judges a mother due to how she's dressed. A teacher named Janine (played by Quinta Brunson) asks, "Why does it matter?" Barbara doesn't have a response. The way the parent dresses doesn't affect anything or anyone negatively. The child arrives at school on time and seems to be a well-adjusted, star pupil. Some differences can be serious, so we should care about them. Others are just a matter of opinion.

What differences in your family are harmful and affect others negatively? *Example: My brother calls his children "stupid" when they make a mistake. I've seen my nephew cry as a result.*

_____

_____

_____

_____

_____

_____

_____

_____

_____

What differences in your family aren't harmful and are simply a matter of opinion?

Example: My brother gives his kids candy, while I wouldn't give that much candy to kids.

_____

_____

_____

_____

_____

_____

_____

_____

TAKE A MOMENT
TO REFLECT

These exercises are meant to help you grow and gain insight. They should feel less like homework and more like self-nurturing.

In this chapter, what has been the most challenging thing for you to reflect on? What caused you to pause? Do you know why?

. . . .

CHAPTER 3

Addiction, Neglect, and Abuse

Some things don't get better with time. A hard thing that isn't talked about enough is not receiving the love you needed in childhood—and accepting that the adults in question still aren't what you need today.

Addiction is challenging for some because it can be stigmatizing if you're the addict, and hard to identify and comprehend if you're someone who suspects addiction. Society's understanding of addiction is starting to shift, but much work still needs to be done to reduce the stigma attached to it and to offer solutions when needed.

Addiction is considered the inability to stop using drugs or alcohol, or to stop gambling, shopping, or engaging in other behaviors that negatively affect your life, at will. It may be an issue when someone can't freely stop behavior that causes negative life consequences or relationship and mental health issues, or is unable to function without the behavior. Many people, however, consider themselves nonaddicts because they're "functional," meaning they're able to work or maintain a relationship. But addiction is complex and doesn't manifest in the same way for every person.

Write your own definition of "addiction." What are the characteristics of someone with a substance-use problem or other addiction?

_____

_____

_____

_____

_____

_____

SUBSTANCES AND OTHER ADDICTIONS

According to the National Institute on Alcohol Abuse and Alcoholism, 14.5 million Americans in 2019 were reportedly addicted to alcohol. Under this umbrella, heavy and binge drinking are included. It's certainly hard to say how many people struggle with substance misuse, because _misuse_ is often underestimated, as only people who encounter governmental or medical systems will be included in statistics.

Marijuana, opioids, prescription pills, and more fall under the definition of "addiction" when a person who has lifestyle consequences cannot stop using a substance. Yet as with any addiction, people aren't typical in their substance use, so it's impossible to fit everybody into a box.

Addiction impacts everyone in a family, whether because of secrets, shame, abuse, or neglect.

Who misused substances in your family when you were growing up?

_____

_____

_____

What were the unspoken rules for dealing with the person misusing substances?

_____

_____

_____

Were substance issues ever discussed openly? If so, what was said?

_____

_____

_____

DEVELOPING A
DEEPER UNDERSTANDING

Addiction is not a choice; it's a behavior pattern that's harmful and difficult to stop. If it were easy to stop, no one would suffer from it. In families, people often believe the person with the addiction has chosen the unhealthy vice over them, without considering why their loved one might have become addicted in the first place.

Consider the entire story—your side and theirs.

FAMILY MEMBER	WHAT HAPPENED TO THEM?	HOW DOES THEIR BEHAVIOR IMPACT YOU AND OTHER FAMILY MEMBERS?	HOW DOES THEIR BEHAVIOR MAKE YOU FEEL?	HOW DO YOU CHOOSE TO INTERACT WITH THEM?

FAMILY MEMBER	WHAT HAPPENED TO THEM?	HOW DOES THEIR BEHAVIOR IMPACT YOU AND OTHER FAMILY MEMBERS?	HOW DOES THEIR BEHAVIOR MAKE YOU FEEL?	HOW DO YOU CHOOSE TO INTERACT WITH THEM?

PROBLEMATIC BEHAVIORS

In recent years, it has become more common to see social media or the excessive use of technology as an addiction. Again, anything that impacts our lifestyle in a negative way could technically be considered an addiction. For instance, if your parents spent the entire evening on social media, didn't give you a meal or check your homework, and didn't ensure you were cared for, social media usage would be considered a problem. Research is conflicting as to whether it constitutes an addiction, with some research from Michigan State University saying that social media addiction impairs decisions in the same way as gambling addiction. Other research from the University of Strathclyde, in Scotland, says that the lifestyle consequences are minimal. It's widely known, however, that social media use can cause reduced productivity, unhealthy social relationships, and decreased life satisfaction.

There are other potentially problematic behaviors such as shopping or tobacco use that can become an issue for individuals and others around them. Behaviors like these can't always be clinically diagnosed, yet they're often still a problem.

You don't need to have a label for something for it to be problematic. In dysfunctional families, things are often downplayed because they're considered "not that big of a deal." In the spaces below, I invite you to make a big deal out of them.

What was actually a big deal, even if it was treated like no big deal?
Example: My father stayed out all weekend, and my mother never seemed upset when he returned. We had no clue where he was. But he was scary, so no one dared to ask him.

_____

_____

_____

_____

• _____

_____

_____

• _____

_____

_____

_____

EXAMPLES OF
PROBLEMATIC REACTIONS

Defensiveness

To protect themselves, people often become defensive when confronted with their issues. They might try to turn it back on you, saying, "But what about what *you* did?" Accountability can be challenging, but it is a gift because it offers knowledge and allows us to consider the truth.

Denial

Family members and the person with the problem may be in denial. It can be more difficult to see what's happening clearly than to deny it.

Blaming Others

Pointing the finger outward is easier than pointing the finger inward.

Emotional Immaturity

Chronological age and emotional age are not the same.

Selfishness

People with substance issues may find it hard to focus on anything outside themselves and their own interests.

Manipulation

To get their needs met, people with substance issues sometimes manipulate others.

What tactics did the addicts in your life use most often?

What tactics felt most harmful?

Did you adopt any of these behaviors?

In dysfunctional families, pretending that everything is normal, including minimizing the problems and deflecting from them, is a coping skill.

What's not being said, and why isn't anyone talking about it?

Families remain dysfunctional when everyone pretends that things are okay. Let's brainstorm.

What topics were off-limits in your family?

_____

_____

_____

_____

_____

Why didn't anyone talk about those topics?

_____

_____

_____

_____

_____

Emotional Neglect

Not being cared for properly is neglect. Emotional neglect is when you're ignored or not allowed to express your feelings. Sometimes, people think they weren't neglected because they were loved. But you can be loved and still not receive the emotional support you need. Everyone's needs are different and based on what feels right to them as an individual.

☐ Your family wasn't there when it mattered.

☐ Your parents/guardians expected kids to be mini versions of themselves.

☐ You felt dismissed emotionally.

☐ At an inappropriate age, you were expected to take care of younger siblings.

☐ You weren't allowed to show vulnerability.

☐ Your parents/guardians were emotionally distant.

☐ Your parents/guardians showed little interest in what you cared about.

☐ Your parents/guardians gave you no rules or structure.

Physical Neglect

It's never a child's fault when they can't care for themselves. It isn't their job. In Viola Davis's memoir, *Finding Me*, she spoke about growing up physically neglected in dilapidated housing, often with no utilities. She was teased and knew that her circumstances weren't okay.

DID YOU EXPERIENCE ANY OF THE FOLLOWING?

☐ You had poor hygiene with little direction or correction from an adult.

☐ You didn't have the appropriate clothing for the weather.

☐ Your clothes were often dirty or worn.

☐ You took over your hygiene needs at a young age.

☐ Your home wasn't clean.

- [ ] You lived in unsafe housing conditions.

- [ ] You experienced frequent evictions.

- [ ] You experienced multiple utility disconnections.

As adults, we can remain haunted by what we went through in childhood. Telling our stories to others who can't relate may feel embarrassing. We want to avoid being pitied or looked down upon. But it is often a first step toward healing.

For example, my client Anita was ashamed to admit that when her family was without water, she and her siblings used their tub as a toilet. This was such a troubling memory that she didn't share it with anyone for a long time. She feared what people would think about her. Rationally, Anita knew that at that time, she didn't have another choice, but she still felt like it reflected poorly on her as an adult.

Verbal Abuse

Name-calling, demeaning, bullying, and threatening are forms of verbal abuse. Using profanity to talk down to children is also verbally abusive. Even when kids are misbehaving, it's never okay to call them names or cuss them out. Words can be a weapon. When people are chronically abused verbally, they often struggle with low self-esteem and feelings of inadequacy.

Physical Abuse

Physical and sexual abuse are illegal in most places. However, many children are abused within families without legal intervention. Hitting, slapping, severe spanking, or whipping with objects are all considered abusive practices. In some families, there is a belief that if children aren't spanked, they won't behave. But children who are spanked still misbehave—and often suffer from it psychologically. There are legal limitations around what is too severe. However, even when spanking occurs within legal limits, it can still be unnecessary and abusive.

Sexual Abuse

There is never an acceptable excuse for the sexual abuse of children. Many things can be sexually abusive to children. Abuse occurs when children are exposed to sexual conversations, touched inappropriately, penetrated, made to perform sex acts, the subject of sexual innuendos, exposed to pornography, and more. Incest within families is an abusive practice of family members engaging in sex with other family members. And I repeat, it is never okay.

Memories of sexual abuse can be hard to manage. Notice I said "manage" rather than "get rid of." The truth is, the memories may always be there, so the goal is for you to have those memories without becoming transfixed by them. Memories aren't just in your thoughts; our senses hold memories too. They manifest in sights, sounds, smells, tastes, and touches. Some things repulse us because of the childhood connection. To this day, I love fries but struggle with eating steak fries. My babysitter was a cold woman who was disengaged from caring for children. She wasn't warm and fuzzy toward my little five-year-old self. I remember repeatedly eating oatmeal and steak fries at her house. When I became a breastfeeding mother, I reclaimed oatmeal because it was supposed to help with my milk supply. But steak fries remain something I've yet to conquer consistently.

You are not what happened to you. Ways to deal with this type of shame include naming what happened, learning to disconnect from it, and relating to it from the perspective of who you are now. Let's practice disentangling the versions of who you were from who you are.

What happened then?

_____

_____

_____

_____

_____

How do you view it now?

_____

_____

_____

_____

What happened then?

_____

_____

_____

_____

How do you view it now?

_____

_____

_____

_____

What happened then?

_____

_____

_____

_____

Who are you now?

_____

_____

_____

_____

_____

Remember that dysfunctional families remain unhealthy when secrets are kept and shame is abundant. The antidote to shame is being deeply honest with yourself about your experiences. As you're moving through this book, cry or yell when you feel like it. I want you to practice letting it out instead of keeping it in.

You need to hear this:

- *You're not crazy. It happened the way you remember it.*

- *It wasn't your fault.*

- *Adults are supposed to protect, not harm.*

- *You aren't acting funny or mean because you no longer want to play along.*

- *You don't have to forgive, forget, and pretend.*

- *Your needs matter as much as everyone else's.*

- *You can give people grace and still not allow them the opportunity to injure you.*

- *Keeping secrets perpetuates the dysfunction.*

- *You did what you needed to survive.*

MANAGING DIFFICULT MEMORIES

I offer clients the opportunity to close their eyes and breathe deeply when something painful resurfaces. Immediately after this happens, name your feeling about it—such as "I'm angry." Being present allows you to be honest with yourself and experience the emotion that's arising, rather than suppressing it.

In this chapter, what has been the most challenging thing for you to reflect on? What caused you to pause? Do you know why?

. . . .

CHAPTER 4

Breaking the Cycle

Sometimes it's easier to pretend to be unaware of the truth
because we don't want to do the hard work of dealing
with conflict and ugly realities within the family.

Many people stay in unhealthy family cycles because they don't know anything different. If there's no awareness of the dysfunction, there will be no change. Outside of what's widely known as dysfunctional, including abuse, neglect, substance abuse, and codependency, there are many other issues that may cause a family system to be unhealthy. Yet breaking free is easier said than done because it brings consequences as well as freedom.

THREE KEY REASONS WHY PEOPLE REMAIN IN UNHEALTHY RELATIONSHIPS

1. Fear of isolation from the family or other negative emotional consequences

2. Lack of clarity on whether there's an issue

3. No clue where to start

Which of these three reasons resonates with you the most, and why?

_____

_____

_____

_____

HOW DYSFUNCTIONAL FAMILIES MAINTAIN THE STATUS QUO

The following are examples of communication styles that often perpetuate cycles of dysfunction in families.

Silent Treatment

This involves refusing to talk to someone while upset as a means of punishment. Healthy boundaries and the silent treatment are not the same. Holding clearly stated boundaries and following through with a consequence is different from being mad, upset, or emotionally unavailable because you want to stonewall the other person.

Example: When Allison asked her father not to drink at her birthday party, she didn't hear from him for six months. She attempted to call him, but he wouldn't respond.

Deflecting

This is intentionally changing the topic or ignoring significant issues because we're uncomfortable or don't want to talk about the topic/issues.

Example: Whenever Jerome would talk about his issues with his brother, their mother would change the subject. This made Jerome feel isolated and alone with his feelings.

Inappropriately Timed Humor

When something is serious, they make light of or use humor to defuse the situation. Comedians often discuss real-life problems and make them funny. However, timing is essential, and everyday life is not a stand-up comedy routine.

Example: Margot's mother was known to have unpredictable crying spells. Margot's brother dealt with it by making jokes about how their mother looked while crying.

Ignoring/Not Talking About Issues

When something big happens, some people don't discuss it and act as though nothing happened.

Example: When Carlos's parents fought, he would hear his mother screaming as she was slapped. The next day, he would notice the bruises on her face, but no one would mention them or acknowledge that anything unusual had taken place.

Enabling (Fixing and Preventing)

A common behavior among loved ones of addicts, enabling can look like upholding the unhealthy behaviors of others, such as purchasing drugs for someone with a drug problem, in order to keep the peace and avoid facing the problem head-on.

Example: Lillian knew her cousin was abusing drugs, but she still loaned him money often. She didn't feel comfortable saying no, even though she felt terrible about his situation.

Cutoffs

This is ending a relationship abruptly, with or without cause.

Example: Amber stopped talking to her mother two months ago with no warning.

Gossiping

This involves sharing mean, harsh, or untrue statements about someone or having conversations with others about confidential situations.

Example: It was commonplace for the Daniel family to be together for the holidays. Whoever was absent would become the topic of discussion. Whatever that person had shared in confidence was recounted to everyone.

Bullying and Manipulation

In dysfunctional families, people often use emotional deception to get what they want from others.

Example: Whenever Jolly told her mom she didn't want to attend church with her, her mother pouted and tried to manipulate her by expressing extreme disappointment and sadness. Often, Jolly gave in because she felt bad.

Aggressiveness

Forceful, mean, confrontational, and demeaning language, including naming-calling, is often used to communicate a need in families where dysfunction festers.

Example: Trevone was often teased by his siblings. They called him "buck-toothed" and made fun of his smile. He couldn't fix his teeth as a child, but it was one of the first things he did as an adult. As a result, he harbored resentment toward his siblings well into adulthood. Trevone's father normalized the teasing, saying his brothers were just poking fun.

Cycles may be present in one generation or across generations. If something is recurring within a generation, it's a cycle too. In your family, what cycles have you observed?

Example: Most of the women in my family are single mothers. There was an energy of "I can do it myself" in the family.

Name your family cycle (whether it appears in one generation or across generations). List recurring patterns you see in your family, whether positive or negative:

- _____

  _____

- _____

  _____

- _____

  _____

- _____

  _____

- _____

  _____

- _____

  _____

- _____

  _____

- _____

  _____

For the cycles listed, which ones would you like to change?

- _____

  _____

- _____

  _____

_____

_____

_____

_____

_____

Becoming a Cycle-Breaker

A cycle-breaker is a person who intentionally breaks the pattern of family dysfunction. When you're the first, you often receive more pushback from other family members because you're challenging the family norms.

WAYS PARENTS HARM CHILDREN LONG-TERM

- Turning a child against the other parent

- Not protecting them from known dangers

- Using them as emotional companions and confidants

- Vicariously living through their child

- Giving them anything they want

- Doing things for them when they can be taught to function independently

- Giving them advice based on what the parents want instead of what's good for the child

RESILIENCE

Resilience is not resistance to suffering. It's the capacity to bend without breaking. Strength doesn't come from ignoring the pain. It stems from knowing that your past self has hurt and your future self will heal. Fortitude is the presence of resolve, not the absence of hardship.

—ADAM GRANT

Strength in the face of adversity—not dodging or ignoring what happened—is resilience. Unfortunately, society has made mental health treatment, speaking up about family problems, and asking for help seem like weaknesses. The truth is that they are all strengths. It's brave to be authentic and put words to what's really going on.

In childhood, the following are protective factors, according to the National Child Traumatic Stress Network. That is, they help a child navigate challenging circumstances beyond their control:

- Relationship with a trusted adult

It's brave to be authentic.

- Regular participation in sports

- Community engagement

- Perceived financial support

- Feeling of safety at home

- Dreams and hopes for the future

- Strong sense of spirituality or religion

- High self-esteem

Did any of these apply to you? If so, did you know you were protecting yourself from your environment?

STRENGTHS ASSESSMENT

1. Circle your strengths in the list below, and use the additional space to add your own.

Brave	Thoughtful	Passionate
Patient	Assertive	Modest
Strong-willed	Helpful	Cooperative
Adventurous	Humorous	Kind
Calm	Flexible	Open-minded

_____

_____

_____

_____

2. What compliments do you receive from others?

_____

_____

_____

_____

_____

_____

3. In your relationships with others, what do you do well?

_____

_____

_____

_____

_____

_____

4. Describe a time when your strengths helped you in your family.

_____

_____

_____

_____

_____

FEELING IS A WAY TO BREAK THE CYCLE

It's healthy and normal to feel more than one way about things, yet it's hard to feel our feelings. When trauma is unfolding or a distressing event is occurring, there isn't time to feel or process. Many of us act or react without thinking. Years, months, or weeks later, we're left with the unprocessed feelings of the past. In this next exercise, I want you to allow yourself to go back and describe both primary and secondary emotions that you felt at the time. Yes, it's still helpful to process those feelings. There's no time limit for working through them. Also allow yourself to feel more than one thing at the same time.

Your primary *emotion in a situation is the first or strongest emotion you feel. Your* secondary *emotion is another emotion you feel at the same time, though perhaps not as strongly or immediately.*

SIGNIFICANT EVENT	PRIMARY FEELING (AT THE TIME)	SECONDARY FEELING (AT THE TIME)

It's okay if a particular feeling stands out or if you feel more than one thing equally.

For the situations above, have your feelings changed over time, perhaps with more information or the passing of time?

SIGNIFICANT EVENT	PRIMARY FEELING (CURRENTLY)	SECONDARY FEELING (CURRENTLY)

Feelings inform us about which wounds are still deep and need our attention. Additionally, they help us discover where we've grown.

- "I am not responsible for other people's feelings."

- "I can care without being consumed."

- "I don't know what's best for others."

- "My needs are important."

- "I can love people and not make myself responsible for solving their problems."

When unhealthy patterns aren't addressed, they persist. How do your family of origin's issues manifest in other relationships in your life?

Example: Erica's mother was competitive and demeaned Erica as a way to have the upper hand. When Erica shared good news with her mother, her mother would dismiss it and talk about ways that she herself had achieved more. Now that she is an adult, Erica has had trust issues with other women, making it difficult for her to create friendships with them.

_____

_____

_____

_____

_____

_____

_____

_____

_____

Family relationships impact not only your overall well-being but also your relationships outside the family. If you want healthier relationships overall, I encourage you to break the cycle.

In this chapter, what has been the most challenging thing for you to reflect on? What caused you to pause? Do you know why?

CHAPTER 5

Moving Beyond Survival Skills

You survive when you maintain the status quo,
but you thrive *when you create a new legacy and trajectory.*

Constance had a complicated relationship with her mother, Laverne. "Self-absorbed" was how Constance often described her mother's behavior. Laverne enjoyed spending time with Constance but insisted on doing things she wanted, not things Constance suggested. As far as Laverne knew, she and Constance had a lot of similarities and Constance loved hearing her mother talk about what was happening in her life.

Laverne started referring to Constance as her best friend when Constance was four years old. Constance always felt in the loop, inappropriately so. She knew far too much about her mother's dating escapades, issues with coworkers, and family problems. Constance often felt that her mother didn't have the emotional capacity to hold her own emotions, because Laverne seemed so fragile. If Constance expressed a tinge of a different opinion or preference, Laverne would give her the silent treatment. Constance learned to keep her opinions to herself.

Laverne demanded closeness. She would drop by unannounced, make plans for the two of them, and call when she knew that Constance would be unavailable, such as when Constance was spending time with friends. Constance was frustrated. However, she realized that she was all her mother ever had. The only way Constance knew how to function in the relationship with her mother was to shrink and comply.

You survive when you keep pace with life, and you *thrive* when you make corrective life choices and move beyond just getting by. When relationships are less than ideal within a family, it's commonly thought that's just how it has to be. In actuality, we can move beyond surviving and instead create something that allows us to be more comfortable, and more truly ourselves.

IT'S COMPLICATED

We often live with multiple truths and uncertainties. Humans feel mixed emotions about many things. Accepting where you are can be more freeing than forcing yourself to solve what no longer works for you. With relationships, allowing unhealthy patterns to continue is a way of surviving in the family system. You don't want to do anything that might disrupt the environment. Having mixed feelings, seeing the problem, and wanting to change, while being okay that everyone else is content with the ways things are, is normal.

You can feel conflicted or guilty and still change your behaviors. Feelings don't have to determine your actions. Allow yourself to be conflicted while also making healthy changes.

When you open yourself up to the possibility that multiple feelings can coexist, it becomes easier for you to acknowledge the positive and negative aspects of your relationships.

Name a few current experiences that you have multiple feelings about. You can list two or more feelings.

CURRENT EXPERIENCE	FEELINGS
I enjoy my job, but I don't like my coworkers.	Happy, annoyed, confused

Leaving things as they are is one option, while trying to change the system is another. Certainty is not a requirement for making a change. Sometimes, the path becomes clear only after you take the first step.

SILENCE IS SURVIVING, NOT THRIVING

When you don't speak up, people can be unaware that there's an issue. To them, the relationship is wonderful—or at least, you seem satisfied with the status quo. Speaking about the problems indicates that you are committed to improving the relationship and desire a more authentic connection with the other person and a healthier reality for yourself.

Let's practice reframing what uncomfortable conversations mean. Hint: "Uncomfortable" does not equal "bad." Create your own list.

UNCOMFORTABLE CONVERSATIONS MAY MEAN

Example: I care about you and want to discuss something that bothers me.

- _____

- _____

- _____

- _____

Questioning Yourself Instead of Examining the Dysfunctional Relationship

REASONS YOU MAY NOT ENJOY SPEAKING TO YOUR PARENTS

- They tell you how to live your life.

- They complain.

- They gossip.

- They have a chronically negative outlook.

- They seem moody or negative or drain your energy.

- They have different life views, and these differences cause arguments.

- They pressure you to do things or show up in ways that make you uncomfortable.

- They don't know you very well and seem uninterested in learning more about you.

- They focus on themselves without showing interest in your life.

Reassure yourself that you aren't making things up. I knew I needed to change something in a problematic family relationship when I started recording my conversations with the person and archiving every text. Gaslighting was their go-to strategy, and I wanted to be clear that I wasn't making things up. Ultimately, it was a huge red flag when I commenced recording conversations; it was a sign that I needed to exit the relationship, not verify everything said.

Pay Attention to Your Red Flags

When I started secretly recording conversations with a family member because I had a feeling they would later deny what they said, I knew something needed to change in my relationship.

I knew something needed to change in the relationship when

- _____

_____

_____

- _____
  _____
  _____

- _____
  _____
  _____

- _____
  _____
  _____

EMOTIONAL DETACHMENT

Before we physically leave relationships, we may first emotionally detach or place emotional boundaries. Sociologist Karl Pillemer has noted that emotional estrangement—separating the emotional parts of who you are with others—is a form of detachment. Remaining silent and not sharing what's happening in your world are two ways to detach emotionally. Use the following checklist to identify how you emotionally detach yourself from others.

☐ You deliberately avoid spending time with them.

- ☐ If they changed, it wouldn't matter anymore.

- ☐ You lack the desire to improve anything to make the relationship work.

- ☐ Almost everything they do seems annoying.

- ☐ You avoid making plans for the future.

- ☐ You feel lonely in their presence.

- ☐ What you used to enjoy with them is now joyless.

Emotional safety is an integral part of feeling healthy in your relationships. When you can't trust that what you tell someone will remain private, your views aren't respected, you are told to "get over it," you are told how to feel or what to think, or your emotions are dismissed, then protective emotional boundaries may be needed.

Write about the emotionally safe relationships you currently have in your life.

_____

_____

_____

_____

_____

Did you have any emotionally safe relationships with family members when you were growing up? If so, write about those relationships here.

_____

_____

_____

_____

_____

_____

_____

_____

_____

_____

_____

When you haven't been able to trust the people closest to you, it can be hard to learn to trust others. Trust is essential for healthy relationships. To thrive, you must learn to trust others.

WHEN YOU EXPERIENCE MULTIPLE UNHEALTHY RELATIONSHIPS, IT'S COMMON TO

- Believe that relationships can't be healthy

- Be suspicious of people being kind to you

- Not trust your instincts

- Struggle to communicate your needs to others because in the past they were ignored or minimized

- Look past red flags because you want to believe that it's not that bad

- Have flashbacks of unhealthy relationship dynamics from the past

- Accept all the responsibility for things not going well

- Want to save others in similar situations even though you're still struggling

- Fear trying again with someone else

Who triggers a strong emotional response in you? Mom, Dad, your sister, your brother . . .

WHO TRIGGERS YOU?	WHAT IS AN EXAMPLE OF THE WAY THEY TRIGGER YOU?

EVERYTHING YOU NEED
MAY NOT COME FROM ONE PLACE

Accept this truth: What you need might be outside of your family. The people who raised you likely took you as far as they could emotionally; it's your responsibility to continue learning what you need, discerning how to get your needs met, and unlearning things that weren't particularly helpful. When family members are unwilling to see themselves and their behavior, it can be re-traumatizing to explain why you're hurt, what they did, and why things are the way they are. People who don't want to be accountable won't be responsible. Adulthood allows you to create a life for yourself outside of what you were taught (or not taught). You are now in the driver's seat. You are parenting yourself. Therefore, nurture yourself and fill in the missing parts. Add relationships that enhance your existence. Refuse to be imprisoned by your past.

> Surviving *is the first step. It means you're getting through the day any way you can even though your emotional needs aren't being met—you're just existing.* Thriving *happens when you have enough support and healing to change your approach to life and start flourishing.*

My mission in life is not merely to survive, but to thrive; and to do so with some passion, some compassion, some humor, and some style.

—MAYA ANGELOU

THRIVERS DO THIS

- Own how they contribute to issues in their relationships

- Ask questions instead of assuming

- Make changes, not excuses

- Create a plan

- Look for support in places outside their families

Surviving involves a lot of thinking fast and moving quickly past your feelings. Releasing yourself from survival mode looks like slowing down to feel the moments you tried to survive. You have time now to be with yourself. Complete these statements:

When I was in survival mode, I couldn't feel . . .

_____

_____

_____

When I was in survival mode, I couldn't say . . .

_____

_____

_____

When I was in survival mode, I likely needed . . .

_____

_____

_____

When I was in survival mode, I was expected to . . .

_____

_____

_____

What might it look like to thrive?

_____

_____

_____

In this chapter, what has been the most challenging thing for you to reflect on? What caused you to pause? Do you know why?

. . . .

CHAPTER 6

Seeing Things as They Are

Acceptance isn't easy,
but it can make life more peaceful.

Acceptance is seeing things as they are while knowing you don't have the power to change what is. But . . .

Acceptance doesn't mean forgiveness.

Acceptance doesn't mean denial.

Maya Angelou famously said, "When people show you who they are, believe them." Unfortunately, we often not only don't believe them, but we also try to make them something they're not.

In relationships, you own your power when you live in the truth of what is and not what could be or what you wish someone else would be.

Here are a few examples of what acceptance looks like in a relationship:

"My mother is not nurturing."

"My father consumes our conversations with his issues and expresses little desire to know more about me."

"My brother competes with me in several aspects of life."

"My cousin is my grandmother's favorite grandchild."

With the understanding of what's true, you can decide how you want to exist in the relationship. For example, you might choose to form relationships with other elders who are more nurturing if your mother isn't a source of nurturing for you.

Name a few things that you accept about members of your family.

Mother: I accept _____

_____

_____

Father: I accept _____

_____

_____

Sibling: I accept _____

_____

_____

Sibling: I accept _____

_____

_____

Extended family member: I accept _____

_____

_____

Extended family member: I accept _____

_____

_____

Extended family member: I accept _____

_____

_____

_____

Extended family member: I accept _____

_____

_____

Other: I accept _____

_____

_____

Other: I accept _____

_____

_____

_____

Other: I accept _____

_____

_____

YOUR FEELINGS MATTER

Countless times, I've said to clients, "I can help the person who is present in my office today; I can't help the people in your life who don't want to change. You are here, and they are not. My job is to help you, not them." While those words offer little comfort, they reflect a truth my clients benefit from hearing.

We can help people only when they want help, not when they don't.

The person reading this book (you) or sitting in front of a therapist is the one who is most likely to change. Identify how you feel about working on the situation, knowing the other person will probably not do their part. I'm offering you an invitation to vent about how you feel about doing the work when you aren't the person causing the issue.

Use the space below to express your feelings. If one feeling doesn't apply, move on to the next statement.

I'm angry because _____

_____

_____

_____

I'm frustrated because _____

_____

_____

I'm resentful because _____

_____

_____

I'm sad because _____

_____

_____

INFORMED RELATIONSHIPS

Once you've accepted a situation, how will you respond differently and act accordingly? You won't achieve peace if you continue to expect people to be different or try to convince them to be different. That will only cause frustration, prolonged grief, anger, and resentment.

Acceptance opens up potential choices. Pull your attention toward what you *can* do when you *can't* change other people.

In my relationship with _____, I can do the following: _____

_____

_____

_____

_____

In my relationship with _____, I can do the following: _____

_____

_____

_____

_____

In my relationship with _____, I can do the following: _____

_____

_____

_____

In my relationship with_____, I can do the following: _____

_____

_____

_____

_____

In my relationship with _____, I can do the following: _____

_____

_____

_____

_____

In my relationship with _____, I can do the following: _____

_____

_____

_____

"Accepting a relationship for what it is doesn't mean taking anything someone else dishes out. My power lies in determining how I want to proceed when the other person demonstrates what they're capable, or incapable, of doing."

Acceptance goes only so far. Some of the things people do to you are abusive and intolerable.

Melanie's grandfather was often mean toward his grandchildren. Although it was the norm in the family to ignore his behavior, Melanie chose not to allow him to be mean to her. She told this to her parents and refused to stop pretending his treatment of her and others was okay.

If you find that a relationship is no longer sustainable, the next chapter will help you release the connection.

HEALTHY RELATIONSHIPS

"Love" is a verb. When the relationships in your family are dysfunctional, love is expressed differently. In your family, how was love expressed?

Complete the statement:

In my family, love was seen as . . .

Example: In my family, love was seen as minimizing my own needs and always being there for others.

WHAT DOES HEALTHY LOVE FEEL LIKE TO YOU?

My List

Healthy love feels like:

- Someone listening after they ask me how I'm doing

- People showing they care by being present with me in challenging moments

- Someone allowing me to feel without telling me what to feel

Create Your Own List

Healthy love feels like:

- _____

- _____

- _____

ROLES DO NOT GUARANTEE HEALTHY RELATIONSHIPS

A role within a family structure doesn't determine the quality of your relationship with a person, nor does the frequency of contact. Someone's role in your life might be that of your sister, but that doesn't mean it's a healthy relationship.

Casey speaks to her mother, Janice, daily. Janice does most of the talking—gossiping about other family members—and complaining consumes the conversations. When Casey attempts to talk, Janice seems uninterested. She changes the subject, doesn't ask follow-up questions, or says, "That's life." Janice calls at least twice a day because Casey is her confidante.

What does the relationship offer Casey? She wants to be connected to her mother because she loves her sense of humor, their shared history, and knowing about family. But she has to decide if it's worth it to her to maintain this complicated relationship that involves so much more taking than giving.

What are your reasons for maintaining your own complicated relationships?

_____

_____

_____

_____

_____

_____

_____

Values that are important to you in nonfamilial relationships can also be applied to family. Lowering your standards "because it's family" isn't healthy for you.

What values/standards have you maintained in friendships or romantic relationships that you've been lenient about with family members?

_____

_____

_____

_____

_____

SEEING MORE CLEARLY

We don't have the option of picking the family we're born into. Some people are born into royalty, and others are born into poverty. Your work involves learning how to exist with the family you have. Wishing things were different doesn't work.

Cognitive distortions often keep us in negative thought patterns about possible family relationships. Here are the most common cognitive distortions about family relationships:

Overgeneralizing: Applying one thought to every family member and every situation.

"No one in my family understands my issues."

Discounting the positive: Seeing only the negative and finding no value in the positive things that occur.

> *Your parents paid for undergraduate college, but they didn't pay for graduate school. In your retelling, you believe they have never helped you with anything.*

Jumping to conclusions: Assuming and acting without evidence.

> *When your sister calls you in the evening on your birthday rather than earlier in the day, you assume she forgot about it.*

Catastrophizing: Believing the worst-case scenario will occur.

> *"If I tell my father how his drinking has affected me, he'll never talk to me again."*

Personalization: Ascribing ownership of all problems to something you did or didn't do.

> *Believing it's your fault that your parents don't get along.*

Control fallacies: Believing you have power over the actions of others.

> *When you don't loan your brother money for gas, you believe it's your fault if he's unable to get to work.*

Fairness fallacies: Expecting things to be fair even when the playing field isn't leveled.

> *"Parents should pay for college. Mine both had jobs and couldn't afford to pay for myself or my siblings to attend college."*

Blaming: Holding others accountable for your feelings or needs.

Your sister left home for college. You're still mad because she abandoned you.

Shoulds: Seeing things as you'd like them to be instead of as they are.

"Mothers should stay home with their children. Mine did not, and that isn't fair."

Emotional reasoning: Allowing your feelings to determine facts.

"My parents chose drugs over me."

Bottom line: Think deeply about your thoughts before behaving as if they are true.

How have you exhibited cognitive distortions about your family?

_____

_____

_____

_____

_____

Cognitive Distortions in Family Relationships

COGNITIVE DISTORTION	PERSONAL EXAMPLE
Overgeneralizing	
Discounting the positive	
Jumping to conclusions	
Catastrophizing	
Personalization	
Control fallacies	
Fairness fallacies	
Blaming	
Shoulds	
Emotional reasoning	

Take a minute to write about the best-case scenario. Often, we focus on what's not likely to happen. In the space below, I invite you to dream about things going well and the possibility of hard conversations evolving into more connected interactions.

If I could have an ideal outcome with _____, **it would look like**

_____

_____

_____

_____

_____

_____

If I could have an ideal outcome with _____, **it would look like**

_____

_____

_____

_____

_____

_____

_____

_____

In this chapter, what has been the most challenging thing for you to reflect on? What caused you to pause? Do you know why?

CHAPTER 7

Deciding to End
When You Can't Mend

When people say, "You have to love your family no matter what,"
they may not understand the "what" that has caused you
to create distance or end a relationship.

What constitutes "enough" is unique for each of us. We decide to leave a relationship when we recognize that the negative effects on our life and mental well-being are too great.

People often stay in unhealthy relationships because there are both positive and negative aspects. Not all negative experiences are equal in impact; some sit with us for a short time, while others reverberate long-term, especially those that are ongoing with few or no signs of improvement. Of course, there are situations that bother us and situations that actually threaten our safety.

For example, Alexis's mother and father always favored her sister, June, who were their firstborn, and had struggled with infertility before having her.

June absorbed the attention and took advantage in a way that left Alexis feeling slighted by all three of them. Alexis worked the most on her relationship with her mother, who constantly compared her with June, took June's side, and dismissed any issues Alexis had with her sister. After speaking with her mother about the issue for years with no results, Alexis decided to step back from their relationship.

Then there's Abraham, who was physically and verbally abused by his father. Whenever his dad was around, Abraham felt uneasy. Even after he reached adulthood, the verbal abuse continued. His father demeaned him, called him names, and justified the abuse. "You were a bad kid," his dad would say, or "If you think what was happening to you was bad, you should've had *my* parents. They beat the crap out of me."

No one can tell you that your "enough" point for ending a relationship or minimizing contact is wrong. They can only speak from their own experience and tolerance level. And tolerance is different for every person. No one has the right to make you experience more of something that's harmful to you.

Let's try to understand how you continue to be affected by the negative aspects of relationships.

FAMILY MEMBER: _____

• *Emotional*

When engaging with this person, I feel _____

_____

_____

_____

• *Physical*

I experience the following physical symptoms (increased heart rate, nausea, sleep issues, etc.): _____

_____

_____

_____

• *Behavioral*

I notice the following changes in my behavior: _____

_____

_____

_____

• *Relationships*

The negative aspects of this relationship affect my other relationships in the following ways: _____

_____

_____

_____

• *Life in general*

The negative aspects of this relationship impact my life in the following ways: _____

_____

_____

_____

I've been dealing with this issue since _____

FAMILY MEMBER: _____

• *Emotional*

When engaging with this person, I feel _____

_____

_____

_____

• *Physical*

I experience the following physical symptoms (increased heart rate, nausea,

sleep issues, etc.): _____

_____

_____

_____

- *Behavioral*

I notice the following changes in my behavior: _____

_____

_____

_____

- *Relationships*

The negative aspects of this relationship affect my other relationships in the following ways: _____

_____

_____

_____

- *Life in general*

The negative aspects of this relationship impact my life in the following ways: _____

_____

_____

_____

I've been dealing with this issue since _____

FAMILY MEMBER: _____

• *Emotional*

When engaging with this person, I feel _____

_____

_____

_____

• *Physical*

I experience the following physical symptoms (increased heart rate, nausea, sleep issues, etc.): _____

_____

_____

_____

- *Behavioral*

I notice the following changes in my behavior: _____

_____

_____

_____

- *Relationships*

The negative aspects of this relationship affect my other relationships in the following ways: _____

_____

_____

- *Life in general*

The negative aspects of this relationship impact my life in the following ways: _____

_____

_____

_____

I've been dealing with this issue since _____

In your problematic family relationships, have you ever felt any of the following?

☐ Obligated to stay in an unhealthy relationship

☐ Fear that ending the relationship would end other relationships

☐ Pressured by others to tolerate more

☐ Concerned for your safety (emotional or physical)

Which of these common reasons for ending a relationship apply to you?

☐ Long-standing trauma

☐ Present-day issues of safety

☐ Emotional abuse

☐ Sexual abuse

☐ Gossiping, gaslighting, or manipulation

☐ Chronic boundary violations

☐ Harmful substance misuse

☐ Frequent disputes

☐ Disagreements about lifestyle, creating a lack of respect

☐ Poor connection

☐ No shared values

☐ The other person's mental health issues hurt you

YOU'VE DONE ALL YOU CAN

A friend once told me, "You've set every boundary possible; there are none left." It wasn't my lack of effort but my relative's unwillingness to do anything differently. Time after time, I forgave, set boundaries, created distance, had hard conversations, and set more boundaries. Yet nothing changed in my relationship with this person. Acceptance involved acknowledging that they were unwilling to change despite my efforts and that their behavior was harmful, not just toward me but also toward others. After the final blow, when they admitted they would not respect my boundaries, I decided to withdraw from the relationship. Before leaving, I tried speaking less frequently with them, but this only made them want to talk to me more. I placed boundaries around what I would and wouldn't share with them, and this made them angry. Whenever I was with them, I felt guarded and anxious. I reached my "enough" point.

With _____, what strategies have you tried to improve the relationship or to remain cordial?

_____

_____

_____

_____

With _____, what strategies have you tried to improve the relationship or to remain cordial?

_____

_____

_____

_____

With _____, what strategies have you tried to improve the relationship or to remain cordial?

_____

_____

_____

_____

With _____, what strategies have you tried to improve the relationship or to remain cordial?

_____

_____

_____

For example, Josephine's mother, Valerie, was an addict for twenty-two years. Valerie wasn't present consistently, so Josephine was raised primarily by her aunt, father, and paternal grandmother. Once Valerie was clean for two years, she tried reconnecting with her daughter. Despite this sobriety, however, Josephine wanted nothing to do with her mother.

Some will say Josephine should have forgiven and moved on. At the same time, Josephine lived without the relationship and didn't see a reason to rebuild.

CHALLENGING THE MESSAGING FROM OTHERS

"You only get one mother." What if your mother hasn't treated you right or isn't treating you right?

"You only get one father." What if your father hasn't treated you right or isn't treating you right?

"It isn't that big of a deal." What if it's a big deal to you?

Perhaps what happened is in the past, but you can still decide to end a damaging relationship. Rekindling a connection with someone who harmed you is often paired with forgiveness. However, you can forgive and choose not to have a relationship with someone.

People will understand your situation on the level at which they comprehend their own life situations. Others may feel compelled to stay in unhealthy relationships, while you can choose to move on. Just as others are free to choose what relationships to operate in, you, too, are free to choose. Not everyone will agree with your decision; when people express opposition, it is imperative to know how to handle it.

What can you say when people disagree with your decision to end a relationship?
Example: I've thought long and hard about my decision. It wasn't taken lightly. You don't have to agree with me, but please don't tell me what to do.

- _____

- _____

- _____

- _____

HOW TO END
A RELATIONSHIP

There is no one "right" way to end a relationship. Sometimes, you may have a conversation in which your intentions are clearly stated, or you might ghost the other person. Other times, they might ghost you, or the relationship may simply mutually subside.

Ghosting Explained

Ghosting is when we leave a relationship without giving the other person a clue as to why. We cut off communication, and we don't answer phone calls, texts, emails, or any other attempts to communicate with us. Telling it like it is can feel aggressive. We might have already told the person everything we think they need to know about the situation (and maybe some stuff they never needed to know). If they refuse to honor our boundaries or to respect us, we might choose to simply walk away with no further explanation.

The ghosted person often feels blindsided by the relationship's end, even if there was a justifiable cause. They might see their behavior as an insufficient reason to end the relationship.

In some situations, however, ghosting may be the safest way out. Physical attacks, gaslighting, and further harm may occur when we try to stay connected or have an honest conversation with certain people. Some people are hard to talk to and likely unwilling to accept anything negative about themselves. You have to decide which people you can speak to directly and which ones you can't.

When possible, of course, try to speak directly to the person to inform them of your intentions. But use your judgment about how to end the relationship based on the person you're dealing with, not a general sense of how relationships "should" end.

Having the Talk

Ending a relationship isn't easy. Sometimes, we overthink what needs to be said and behave as though we need to provide people with an exit interview. There are many creative ways to let someone know we want the relationship to end without giving them a PowerPoint presentation of all the reasons it isn't working. If you feel the need to tell someone as much, you also need to ask yourself some questions:

- Do I want to tell them all this for my benefit or theirs?

- Is it helpful to this person to know all of this?

- What is the intended outcome of sharing this with them?

Of course, when you're the one someone is ending a relationship with, you might wish you knew why. Since you know how that feels, you might be compelled to give someone the reasons why you want to end the relationship with them. Just remember how hard it is to accept the "why" that's given to us.

If you don't want to be in a relationship with someone, however, you don't have to be. You aren't required to explain, and an explanation may not be welcome. What you think is valuable information may not be to someone else. You may think what you're sharing is helpful, but that doesn't mean it will be received that way.

We can't control how people feel or what information they think is important to receive or share. Our work is to end relationships gracefully and deal with our own grief, relief, or other feelings.

Telling someone that you no longer want to be in a relationship with them might be offensive, yet you still need to say it. Just focus on finding the right words to cause the smallest amount of damage when you're saying something the other person won't like.

Expecting someone not to have any response or expecting them to have a positive response to something they don't want to hear will set you up for failure. People are entitled to their feelings and to their response. You are not, however, required to listen to them if they are abusive.

WHAT YOU SHOULD SAY WHEN ENDING A RELATIONSHIP

- "For my well-being, I need to end this relationship."

- "I see how hard you're trying to make this work. The relationship isn't working for me, and I want us to separate."

- "This is really hard for me to say: I don't want to be in this relationship anymore."

- "I think it's important for me to take some time to myself and reflect on our relationship. I need some space to really think about if I want to continue our relationship."

- "I've tried to make this work, but I don't want to fight anymore to keep us together."

- "My vision for my life has changed, and I no longer want this relationship."

Let's Practice

What do you feel comfortable saying? Keep your statements short and sweet. Remember that this isn't the time to change the other person; you're releasing the relationship.

_____

_____

• _____

_____

_____

• _____

_____

_____

Direct communication can be in person or via text, email, or letter. In-person communication is touted as the gold standard, but don't stress yourself out trying to find the perfect time to have the conversation face-to-face. The goal is to say it, in whatever form that takes. If you choose to have the conversation via text, email, or letter, be clear, and minimize back-and-forth engagement. Don't start an argument, and don't join one.

GRIEVING

There's grief in ending a relationship, even when it needs to end or when you initiated the ending. Not every situation improves, and some relationships don't have a happy ending. It's sad to move forward when you wish things were different—and it's important to feel the emotions that come up for you.

There is no appropriate rhythm to grief; it's complex. It's normal to feel fine one moment and remember what you lost the next. Experiencing day-to-day life without the other person will feel different. There will be anger, sadness, fond memories, and painful ones.

Your experience with grief will be unique to you. Suffering happens moment-to-moment, not day-to-day. The world will move around you, and people won't remember what you're going through or feeling. You will be different, but you don't have to fully process and put away those feelings in order to move forward.

Process how you feel after ending a family relationship.

After ending my relationship with _____, I feel _____.

I have memories of them when _____

_____

_____

After ending my relationship with _____, I feel _____.

I have memories of them when _____

_____

_____

After ending my relationship with _____, I feel _____.

I have memories of them when _____

_____

_____

ENGAGING AFTER YOU'VE SEVERED TIES
OR DECREASED FREQUENCY

If you've ended a relationship with someone in your family, you may see or hear about the person from time to time. You might choose to speak to them as you would everyone else in the room, or you might minimize contact altogether.

What feels comfortable for you?

When I see _____, I will _____

_____

_____

_____

When I see _____, I will _____

_____

_____

_____

When I see _____, I will _____

_____

_____

When someone talks to me about _____, I will _____

_____

_____

When someone talks to me about _____, I will _____

_____

_____

When someone talks to me about _____, I will _____

_____

_____

You can't control someone else's relationship with another person.
You can't stop a person from reaching out to you.
You can't make people change.

List what you *can* control in your relationships with others.

_____

_____

_____

_____

_____

_____

_____

_____

_____

_____

In this chapter, what has been the most challenging thing for you to reflect on? What caused you to pause? Do you know why?

CHAPTER 8

Creating a Tool Kit for Difficult Conversations

Awareness is what saves us from repeating patterns.
Understanding your story is a process that unfolds over time,
and your story is constantly evolving.

We all want to get better and do better, but how? Knowing where to begin is the biggest challenge when we want to start new practices and habits in our family relationships. Making unhealthy relationships healthier requires conversations that might make us feel uncomfortable.

No matter how hard a conversation is, I know that on the other side
of that difficult conversation lies peace. Knowledge. An answer is
delivered. Character is revealed. Truces are formed. Misunderstandings
are resolved. Freedom lies across the field of the difficult conversation.
And the more difficult the conversation, the greater the freedom.

—SHONDA RHIMES, *YEAR OF YES*

Simply put, the discomfort will come before the peace.

WHEN PEOPLE ARE EMOTIONALLY IMMATURE, THEY MAY

- Refuse to accept responsibility

- Treat you poorly when they are upset

- Share their issues about you with others, but not with you

- Deny saying things that you know only they could've said

- Try to get you to forgive them by claiming that you're overreacting

- Curse you out or yell when you bring up issues

- Encourage you to dislike the people they dislike

- Spread malicious gossip

- Believe they are never wrong

- Chronically offer unsolicited and unhealthy advice

- Become defensive when corrected

- See little value in reconsidering their behavior

Emotionally immature people don't have the ability to properly regulate their emotions based on the situation. Humans start life dysregulated and learn to regulate their emotions with proper teaching, modeling, and support. Due to generational patterns of dysfunction, some adults may not have had appropriate models for emotional regulation. Getting older doesn't necessarily improve someone's ability to regulate their emotions.

Complete the following statements.

While I was growing up, adults modeled the following regulation skills:

_____

_____

_____

My expectation of adults communicating was

_____

_____

_____

Recently, _____ responded in a dysregulated manner by exhibiting the following:

_____

_____

_____

Recently, _____ responded in a dysregulated manner by exhibiting the following:

_____

_____

_____

Recently, _____ responded in a dysregulated manner by exhibiting the following:

_____

_____

_____

WISDOM IS NOT EARNED WITH AGE ALONE

An old fool starts out as a young fool. Some people do not mature with age. As the person who notices an issue with emotional maturity, you will have to practice being the wise one. Wisdom involves refusing to join people on their level. Allowing someone to be dysregulated while you remain regulated is what you can manage.

Some people do not mature with age.

Some family members may be known for how they respond, so it's helpful to plan how you can respond to them.

If _____ becomes dysregulated, I will _____

_____.

If _____ becomes dysregulated, I will _____

_____.

If _____ becomes dysregulated, I will _____

_____.

When we want to have difficult conversations and say hard things, it's natural to have ambivalent feelings. But ambivalence should not stop us from saying difficult things. Be compassionate about the needs of others while you're also there for yourself. Own your own story, make changes, and say what you need to say even if others disagree with it.

HOW TO START HARD CONVERSATIONS

Dylan wanted to tell his mom that he was spending the holidays with his partner. His mother knew he was gay, but this was the first time he ever mentioned dating someone. Dylan pondered whether calling, texting, or speaking to her in person would be best. Since they lived in different states, an in-person conversation would mean waiting until their next visit. He wanted to get it over with. But the more he thought about the conversation, the more anxious he became.

If you're questioning whether to call, text, email, or speak to someone in person, the best option is the one that will get you to have the conversation. The goal is to speak up. If you're only able to speak up via text, do that. If you want to wait until you're in front of the person, do that. What's most helpful is what you'll actually do, not what's perceived as best practice. When a person doesn't want to hear something, there's no perfect method for making what you need to say less painful.

It can be helpful to process how it has felt for you to have information delivered through various mediums, but be aware that others might feel differently.

In the past, when I read troubling news via text, I felt _____

_____.

In the past, when I read something I didn't want to hear via email, I felt _____

_____.

When someone called me and told me something I didn't want to hear, I felt _____

_____.

When someone spoke to me in person about something I didn't want to hear, I felt ____

_____.

Depending on the modality, did you feel the same or different?

Was there less pain based on the modality?

What do you assume to be someone's preference?

HOW TO FIGHT FAIR

- Decide if the conversation you want to have is truly worth having. Are you pointing out an issue that the person isn't capable of resolving? Are you stating a problem along with a solution? Presenting a problem without a solution often creates another problem. The people with the problem seldom have the solution.

- Mention what you have in common and why you're having the conversation.

    "This relationship is important to me, and that's why I want to talk about _____."

    "We agree on some things, but not _____
    _____."

- Use "I" statements, because you sound accusatory when you say "*You* did this" or "*You* said that." Regardless of the other person's behavior, it's really about you and how you feel about the situation.

DIFFICULT THINGS TO DISCUSS IN DYSFUNCTIONAL FAMILY RELATIONSHIPS

- Financial abuse, opening credit cards, and placing bills in a person's name without their permission

- Never paying someone back after borrowing money

- Spreading lies about a family member to support a narrative

- Favoring one child while neglecting the emotional needs of the others

- Demanding to know everything about a family member's life

- Shaming people for being honest about experiences within the family

MAKE A LIST OF HARD TOPICS YOU WOULD LIKE TO DISCUSS
WITH YOUR FAMILY

- _____

- _____

- _____

- _____

- _____

- _____

- _____

- _____

- _____

- _____

- _____

- _____

RESPECT DOES NOT
REQUIRE AGREEMENT

When I was growing up, I knew not to question what adults said. I didn't understand or agree with all the rules, but I respected them. You can be respected without convincing others to agree with you.

WHEN YOU WANT TO END A CIRCULAR CONVERSATION, PRACTICE SAYING THE FOLLOWING:

- "We don't share the same point of view, and that's okay. Let's move forward knowing how we each feel about the situation."

- "I respect your opinion, and I hope something I said resonated with you."

- "What are some solutions we can use to prevent this issue in the future?"

- "We are starting to restate what we've already said. Let's stop now and return to this when we have something new to add."

- "To prevent this from happening in the future, I would like _____ _____."

People don't love us perfectly. Loving someone doesn't mean knowing their every need or never making a mistake. It's a respectful willingness to learn and grow because we care enough to do so.

FIVE THINGS THAT IMPROVE RELATIONSHIPS

1. Emotional honesty: "I'm upset."

2. Compassionate feedback: "I can hear that you're hurting."

3. Staying committed to our promises

4. Managing our output (how we contribute to the relationship)

5. Sticking to the facts (not assuming)

What did you do when you had problems with certain family members as a child, and how can you handle problems with them as an adult?
Example: As a child, when I had a problem with my mom, I would scream and cry. When I have a problem with her now, I can calmly explain my point of view and end the conversation if she becomes disrespectful.

As a child, when I had a problem with _____, I would _____

_____

_____

When I have a problem with them now, I can _____

_____

_____

As a child, when I had a problem with _____, I would _____

_____

_____

When I have a problem with them now, I can _____

_____

_____

As a child, when I had a problem with _____, I would _____

_____

_____

When I have a problem with them now, I can _____

_____

TIMING

There is no perfect time, but there may be a bad time. The best time to address an issue is in the moment. If you can't do so in the moment, do it soon after. Calling and messaging someone the next day with your grievance and new expectation is fine. If you wait too long, however, it might be challenging for the other person to recall the problem that you remember, and it can be perceived as overreacting or even obsessing.

If you do need to bring up something from the past, though, acknowledge the issue, how it affects you now, and what you expect or will change moving forward.

Complete the following statements:

Who would you like to address? _____

In the past, _____

_____

_____

This impacts our relationship in the following ways: _____

_____

_____

_____

Moving forward, _____

_____

_____

_____

Who would you like to address? _____

In the past, _____

_____

_____

This impacts our relationship in the following ways: _____

_____

_____

_____

Moving forward, _____

_____

_____

Who would you like to address? _____

In the past, _____

_____

_____

This impacts our relationship in the following ways: _____

_____

_____

_____

Moving forward, _____

_____

_____

CALLING IN REINFORCEMENTS

Therapy is a wonderful way to receive support while working through family problems. Common therapies for family issues include emotionally focused therapy, interpersonal family therapy, cognitive behavioral therapy, acceptance and commitment therapy, and solution-focused or talk therapy. Finding a therapist who is familiar with how to work with people with family issues is more important than finding someone who works within a specific modality, however.

Individual Therapy

Whether your family attends or not, it's a good idea to have someone help you sort through the issues within your family. Common topics include what's hard to live with, what drama is currently unfolding, and how it feels to be the only one changing. The hour in therapy each week can be a supportive process to assist you with moving through changes and stuck points in your family.

Family Therapy

Taking the family to therapy is helpful when everyone is willing to talk through issues. Sometimes, a family member will attend therapy under the guise of trying to be proved right, however. If that's an ulterior motive, more problems may arise. Healthy goals include the following:

- Clarity
- Understanding each other
- Setting new boundaries
- Exploring issues as they arise

Couples Therapy

Family relationships impact the couple dynamic, so it can be helpful to attend therapy with your partner while either or both of you work through these issues. Couples therapy can be a supportive space for you or your partner to highlight how family dynamics continue to permeate the couple dynamic.

RECONCILIATION: WHAT'S NEXT?

When you rekindle a family relationship, do so with the intention that things will be different. Change your perspective or behave with new boundaries. Returning to an unhealthy or harmful situation when nothing has changed will only repeat the past.

For example, Mia terminated her relationship with her sister, Jasmine, after many years of sibling rivalry. Jasmine constantly competed with Mia and tried to turn others against her. Four years ago, Mia initiated an estrangement after Jasmine crashed Mia's car and refused to help with the deductible. Two years later, however, Mia missed her sister. So she called her, and everything picked up where they had left off. Mia expected Jasmine to have changed during that passage of time, but the disputes, jealousy, and gossip to other family members remained the same.

THESE ARE NOT REASONS TO RETURN TO AN UNHEALTHY RELATIONSHIP

- You miss the person.

- They asked you to come back.

- You hope they have changed.

- You convince yourself that perhaps it wasn't so bad.

- You think it might be different this time.

- You share a lot of fond memories.

- "Time heals all wounds."

- You have forgiven them and want to forget.

- You're sure there's potential there.

From the previous list, which reason(s) have you used to allow someone back into your life, and how did it work out?

When you're ready or contemplating reconciliation, complete the following assessment:

I'm considering reconnecting with _____ because _____

_____

_____

_____

The relationship ended, or we have talked, because _____

_____

_____

_____

My new view of the situation is _____

_____

_____

_____

I will behave differently by doing the following: _____

_____

_____

_____

I'm considering reconnecting with _____ because _____

_____

_____

_____

The relationship ended, or we have talked, because _____

_____

_____

_____

My new view of the situation is _____

_____

_____

_____

I will behave differently by doing the following: _____

_____

_____

_____

I'm considering reconnecting with _____ because _____

_____

_____

_____

The relationship ended, or we have talked, because _____

_____

_____

_____

My new view of the situation is _____

_____

_____

_____

I will behave differently by doing the following: _____

_____

_____

_____

WAYS I CAN TAKE CARE OF MYSELF AFTER A HARD CONVERSATION

Example: Rewatch my favorite episode of Curb Your Enthusiasm.

- _____

- _____

- _____

- _____

- _____

- _____

In this chapter, what has been the most challenging thing for you to reflect on? What caused you to pause? Do you know why?

CHAPTER 9

Practicing Healthier Relationships

*The truth is that no distraction, vice, or other magic bullet
will help you get over emotions you're still processing.*

Relationship skills are not innate. They are cultivated from experience and are based on what each person needs. In dysfunctional family relationships, love is defined as loyalty, even when you're harmed. In this case, your family expects unlimited forgiveness, weak boundaries, and the willingness to quickly forget the harm caused by others.

Despite what the pop songs say, love is not all you need. Love alone is not enough. People can love you and still hurt you. They can love you and still not love you in the way you desire to be loved. Love is not mind reading. It requires clear communication and emotional presence. It's clearly stating your needs and not playing games.

List the practices that make you feel loved, seen, and respected in relationships:

Example: I feel loved when people listen to understand instead of waiting to reply and dispute.

I feel loved when people honor my boundaries.

I feel loved when people respect that everyone is not the same.

I feel loved when _____.

I feel loved when _____.

I feel loved when _____.

I feel loved when _____.

I feel loved when _____.

I feel loved when _____.

I feel loved when _____.

List what hasn't felt loving in your relationships:

Example: Being gossiped about doesn't feel loving to me.

Being told that I'm a bad person because I refuse to be used doesn't feel loving to me.

_____ doesn't feel loving to me.

_____ doesn't feel loving to me.

_____ doesn't feel loving to me.

_____ doesn't feel loving to me.

_____ doesn't feel loving to me.

_____ doesn't feel loving to me.

_____ doesn't feel loving to me.

RESENTMENT
HARMS RELATIONSHIPS

Withholding an issue and letting it fester is one of the most significant dangers in relationships. Passive-aggressiveness is rooted in resentment, and many times cutoffs stem from such resentment. We often choose not to share what's bothering us because of feelings of shame. Somehow, we think pretending not to be bothered is a better solution than directness. But avoiding difficult conversations only leads to resentment, which can cause backhanded compliments, grudge holding, sabotaging, meanness, and constant conflict in a relationship.

For example, Bishop was six years older than his sister, Liza. When she came along, all attention was shifted to her. People rarely doted on Bishop the way they doted on his sister, so Bishop resented Liza. As a result, they never developed a close bond.

You can't fix the past, but you can choose to do something different in the present.

Example: Hosting gatherings that are more stressful than fun.

Not speaking up when my father forgets to call me on my birthday.

- _____

- _____

- _____

- _____

- _____

- _____

- _____

- _____

- _____

- _____

MORE THAN ONE THING
CAN BE TRUE

People aren't all bad, even when they do some things that are hurtful and wrong. Noticing the fullness of a person can help deepen your compassion for them. However, while seeing the other person's feelings, don't forget about your own. Tend to yourself while also considering others. "And" statements are a great way to allow for nuance in your observations of others. Let's practice a few "and" statements:

Example: My father wasn't there for me when I was growing up, and he's trying to be there for me now.

My grandmother guilt-trips me for not calling her more often, and she's always excited to hear from me.

- _____

- _____

- _____

- _____

Responding in the moment is the best way to stop behavior and prevent future issues. Perhaps you didn't say anything last time. The next time something is said or done, what will you say to prevent it from happening again in the future?

For instance, Tammie wanted to spend time with her friends when she returned from college. When she came home during breaks the last few times, her mother listed the plans she had made for their time together.

What could Tammie say to prevent this issue from occurring again?

_____

_____

_____

Devon's aunt often embellished details and told creative stories about other family members. She called them "white lies." Devon enjoyed his aunt, who was like a surrogate parent to him, but he didn't like how she spoke about others.

What could Devon say to his aunt when she starts embellishing details again?

_____

_____

_____

What situation can you consider from your own life, and how you will respond next time?

_____

_____

_____

_____

_____

_____

_____

_____

_____

_____

_____

RELATIONSHIPS WITH YOUR PARENTS

Parent-child relationships change over time. In a recent talk with Dr. Joshua Coleman, author of *Rules of Estrangement*, he stated that in his research it's been found that parents feel more attached to their adult children than adult children feel to their parents. With this in mind, parents must do things differently to maintain connections with their adult children, and it's helpful when they are accountable for their past actions.

What makes it difficult for you to talk to your parents? Use the checklist below.

☐ They become defensive.

☐ They make everything about them.

☐ They one-up your stories.

☐ They share your business with others.

☐ They aren't good listeners.

☐ They tell you what to do instead of listening.

☐ They give bad advice.

☐ They blame the issue on you.

☐ They become combative.

☐ They assume they know what's best.

Describe a time when you tried to share a grievance with your parents. How did it go?

_____

_____

_____

_____

_____

Despite how they respond, it's still important for you to advocate for yourself, even when it's difficult to speak up. It can be helpful to let them know that you're bringing the issue to their attention because you want to maintain or repair the relationship.

Keep the following list in mind, but don't allow it to stop you from advocating for yourself.

IT'S HARD TO BE RAISED BY ADULTS WHO

- Told you to do as they said but modeled the opposite

- Ignored your emotional needs

- Prioritized what things looked like on the outside

- Gave you the silent treatment but shared everything you said to them with others

- Believed their needs mattered more than yours

- Gave you too many adultlike responsibilities

- Made you feel responsible for taking care of them

- Seemed one way privately and another way publicly

BIG QUESTION:
Are you afraid of your parents? If so, why?

_____

_____

_____

_____

_____

_____

_____

If you feel afraid, will you face similar consequences for speaking up as you did in the past? What might be different this time?

_____

_____

_____

_____

_____

_____

_____

Describe the current issues in the relationship:

_____

_____

_____

_____

Describe the past issues in the relationship:

_____

_____

_____

_____

What are you waiting to hear from your parent(s)?

Example: I would like my parents to apologize and mend their contentious relationship following their divorce.

_____

_____

_____

Is this desire realistic based on the person(s) involved?

Example: My parents may never get along because they are still deeply hurt by each other's actions.

_____

_____

_____

What can you do in this situation?

Example: I can let my parents know that I don't want to hear them bad-mouth each other.

_____

_____

_____

What are you waiting to hear from your parent(s)?

_____

_____

_____

_____

Is this desire realistic based on the person(s) involved?

_____

_____

_____

_____

What can you do in this situation?

_____

_____

_____

_____

What are you waiting to hear from your parent(s)?

_____

_____

_____

Is this desire realistic based on the person(s) involved?

_____

_____

_____

What can you do in this situation?

_____

_____

_____

RELATIONSHIPS WITH YOUR SIBLINGS

What makes it difficult for you to talk to your siblings? Use the checklist below.

- ☐ They become defensive.

- ☐ They make everything about them.

- ☐ They one-up your stories.

- ☐ They share your business with others.

- ☐ They aren't good listeners.

- ☐ They tell you what to do instead of listening.

- ☐ They give bad advice.

- ☐ They blame the issue on you.

- ☐ They become combative.

- ☐ They assume they know what's best.

Describe a time when you tried to share a grievance with your sibling(s).
How did it go?

_____

_____

_____

_____

Describe the current issues in the relationship:

_____

_____

_____

_____

Describe the past issues in the relationship:

_____

_____

_____

_____

What are you waiting to hear from your sibling(s)?

_____

_____

_____

_____

Is this desire realistic based on the person(s) involved?

_____

_____

_____

_____

What can you do in this situation?

_____

_____

_____

_____

What are you waiting to hear from your sibling(s)?

_____

_____

_____

_____

Is this desire realistic based on the person(s) involved?

_____

_____

_____

_____

What can you do in this situation?

_____

_____

_____

_____

RELATIONSHIPS WITH
YOUR GROWN CHILDREN

What makes it difficult for you to talk with your children? Use the checklist below.

- ☐ They become defensive.

- ☐ They make everything about them.

- ☐ They don't apologize when they're in the wrong.

☐ They share your business with others.

☐ They aren't good listeners.

☐ They tell you what to do instead of listening.

☐ They expect you to provide for them even when they can provide for themselves.

☐ They blame the issue on you.

☐ They become combative.

☐ They assume they know what's best.

Describe a time when you tried to share a grievance with your child/children. How did it go?

_____

_____

_____

_____

_____

_____

What are you waiting to hear from your child/children?

_____

_____

_____

_____

Is this desire realistic based on the person(s) involved?

_____

_____

_____

_____

What can you do in this situation?

_____

_____

_____

_____

What are you waiting to hear from your child/children?

_____

_____

_____

_____

Is this desire realistic based on the person(s) involved?

_____

_____

_____

_____

What can you do in this situation?

_____

_____

_____

_____

RELATIONSHIPS WITH YOUR EXTENDED FAMILY: GRANDPARENTS, AUNTS, UNCLES, AND COUSINS

What makes it difficult for you to talk to extended family? Use the checklist below.

- ☐ They become defensive.

- ☐ They make everything about them.

- ☐ They one-up your stories.

- ☐ They share your business with others.

- ☐ They aren't good listeners.

- ☐ They tell you what to do instead of listening.

- ☐ They give bad advice.

- ☐ They blame the issue on you.

- ☐ They become combative.

- ☐ They assume they know what's best.

Describe a time when you tried to share a grievance with extended family. How did it go?

_____

_____

_____

_____

_____

_____

Describe the current issues in the relationship:

_____

_____

_____

_____

Describe the past issues in the relationship:

_____

_____

_____

_____

What are you waiting to hear from your _____?

_____

_____

_____

_____

Is this desire realistic based on the person(s) involved?

_____

_____

_____

_____

What can you do in this situation?

_____

_____

_____

_____

What are you waiting to hear from your _____?

_____

_____

_____

_____

Is this desire realistic based on the person(s) involved?

_____

_____

_____

_____

What can you do in this situation?

_____

_____

_____

_____

RELATIONSHIPS WITH YOUR IN-LAWS

What makes it difficult for you to talk to your in-laws? Use the checklist below.

- ☐ They become defensive.

- ☐ They make everything about them.

- ☐ They one-up your stories.

- ☐ They share your business with others.

- ☐ They aren't good listeners.

- ☐ They tell you what to do instead of listening.

- ☐ They give bad advice.

- ☐ They blame the issue on you.

- ☐ They become combative.

- ☐ They assume they know what's best.

Describe a time when you tried to share a grievance with your in-law(s).
How did it go?

_____

_____

_____

_____

_____

_____

_____

Describe the current issues in the relationship:

_____

_____

_____

_____

Describe the past issues in the relationship:

_____

_____

_____

_____

What are you waiting to hear from your in-law(s)?

_____

_____

_____

_____

Is this desire realistic based on the person(s) involved?

_____

_____

_____

_____

What can you do in this situation?

_____

_____

_____

_____

What are you waiting to hear from your in-law(s)?

_____

_____

_____

_____

Is this desire realistic based on the person(s) involved?

_____

_____

_____

_____

What can you do in this situation?

_____

_____

_____

_____

RELATIONSHIPS WITH BLENDED-FAMILY MEMBERS

What makes it difficult for you to talk to your blended family? Use the checklist below.

- ☐ They become defensive.

- ☐ They make everything about them.

- ☐ They share your business with others.

- ☐ They aren't good listeners.

- ☐ They tell you what to do instead of listening.

- ☐ They blame the issue on you.

- ☐ They become combative.

- ☐ They assume they know what's best.

- ☐ They treat you (or your kids) as outsiders and exclude you.

- ☐ Or, conversely, they're so focused on maintaining harmony that they refuse to talk through conflicts.

Describe a time when you tried to share a grievance with your blended-family member(s). How did it go?

_____

_____

_____

_____

_____

_____

Describe the current issues in the relationship:

_____

_____

_____

_____

_____

Describe the past issues in the relationship:

_____

_____

_____

_____

What are you waiting to hear from your _____?

_____

_____

_____

_____

Is this desire realistic based on the person(s) involved?

_____

_____

_____

_____

What can you do in this situation?

_____

_____

_____

_____

What are you waiting to hear from your _____?

_____

_____

_____

_____

Is this desire realistic based on the person(s) involved?

_____

_____

_____

_____

What can you do in this situation?

_____

_____

_____

_____

In this chapter, what has been the most challenging thing for you to reflect on? What caused you to pause? Do you know why?

CHAPTER 10

Closure

You are the change you wish to see in your family.

Ll family relationships come with challenges. We can't control others, but we *can* learn to manage common issues and respond in emotionally mature ways (most of the time). When you are the person who has the issue with the way things are, you always have the option to change how you show up in the relationship—or decide not to show up at all.

MAKE SPACE FOR COMPLICATED EMOTIONS

Anger is not bad, but how you process it can be.

Frustration is not bad, but how you process it can be.

Learning how to process your feelings when you're angry, upset, frustrated, or sad about an interaction with a family member helps defuse uncomfortable interactions, and can help you stay on track with your larger goals for the relationship going forward.

UNHEALTHY WAYS TO PROCESS FEELINGS	HEALTHY WAYS TO PROCESS FEELINGS
Pull in other family members to share your side of the story and get them on your side.	Go for a walk to cool down.

Sometimes in our attempts to help people who are unhealthy or dysfunctional, we try to give them the tools that worked for us before they are ready to receive them. We may believe that if we share the same book or podcast or strategy that had a positive impact on us that it will do the same for them; but just because we are in a place of healing doesn't mean that they are too.

We may give someone a resource to help them make changes, and they may get a completely different message from it. They may be able to notice dysfunction in others but not be ready to see it in themselves. We can't force a person to be ready, no matter how many tools we give them. We each have to make the decision to change and to heal on our own.

Signs that a person may be ready to change:

- They ask you questions about your healing process.

- They comment positively on the ways you have changed.

- They are using different language than they were previously.

What changes are you ready to make in your relationships?

_____

_____

_____

_____

What changes in behaviors have you seen demonstrated by others?

_____

_____

_____

_____

_____

Expecting change from the person who doesn't see the problem leaves you stuck.

Expecting change from the person who created the problem leaves you stuck.

Expecting change from the person who is okay with things as they are will leave you stuck.

Keep in mind that we all backslide sometimes. We can be really hard on ourselves when we slip back into old behaviors we thought we had overcome. Just because you have a new, elevated way of thinking and managing your emotions doesn't mean your old way of being won't ever resurface. That old part of us that can be petty or vindictive or easily activated may pop up from time to time. When that former version shows up, it doesn't mean you aren't doing the work. It just means we won't always get it right.

Being a new version of yourself may look like:

- Noticing when you've fallen into old patterns

- Catching yourself before you engage in behaviors you've outgrown

- Self-correcting when you realize you acted out of alignment with who you want to be

Growth is not perfection. Growth is being aware of our mistakes and taking steps to course-correct when necessary.

Sometimes we want to forget our former selves—who we used to be and what we used to do. We don't want anyone else to know either, because we think they will judge us or diminish us. When I tell people about some of my hot-mess moments, they can hardly believe it, but that's who I was, and that's still part of who I am. That honesty doesn't take anything away from who I've become.

The Old You and the New You are both you. Leave space for all of yourself.

*In this book, **what has been the most challenging thing for you to reflect on**? What caused you to pause most often? Do you know why?*

What are some hard truths you learned about your family?

You are the solution. While all the responsibility isn't on you, you *do* hold a lot of power in changing your relationships with others. The work is ongoing. I wish you courage, resilience, and patience as you navigate these complex relationships—and create the positive change you deserve.

You are the solution.

Notes/Thoughts

Notes/Thoughts

Notes/Thoughts

_____

_____

_____

_____

_____

_____

_____

_____

_____

_____

_____

_____

_____

Notes/Thoughts

_____

_____

_____

_____

_____

_____

_____

_____

_____

_____

_____

_____

Notes/Thoughts

Notes/Thoughts

Notes/Thoughts

Further Reading

Carrera, Pilar, and Luis Oceja. "Drawing Mixed Emotions: Sequential or Simultaneous Experiences?" *Cognition and Emotion* 21, no. 2 (2007). https://doi .org/10.1080/02699930600557904.

Coleman, Joshua. *Rules of Estrangement: Why Adult Children Cut Ties and How to Heal the Conflict.* New York: Harmony, 2021.

Davis, Viola. *Finding Me.* New York: HarperOne, 2022.

Meshi, Dar, Anastassia Elizarova, Andrew Bender, and Antonio Verdejo-Garcia. "Excessive Social Media Users Demonstrate Impaired Decision Making in the Iowa Gambling Task." *Journal of Behavioral Addictions* 8, no. 1 (2019). https://doi .org/10.1556/2006.7.2018.138.

Pillemer, Karl. *Fault Lines: Fractured Families and How to Mend Them.* New York: Avery, 2020.

University of Strathclyde. "Is Social Media Use a Potentially Addictive Behavior? Maybe Not." *ScienceDaily*, April 20, 2021. https://www.sciencedaily.com/releases /2021/04/210420121443.htm.

About the Author

Nedra Glover Tawwab, MSW, LCSW, is the author of the *New York Times* bestsellers *Drama Free* and *Set Boundaries, Find Peace*, and *The Set Boundaries Workbook*. A licensed therapist and sought-after relationship expert, she has practiced relationship therapy for more than fifteen years. In addition to hosting the podcast *You Need to Hear This*, Nedra has appeared as an expert on *Good Morning America*, *CBS Mornings*, *The Breakfast Club*, and elsewhere. On her popular Instagram account (@NedraTawwab), she shares practices, tools, and reflections for mental health. Nedra lives in Charlotte, North Carolina, with her family.

Also by Nedra Glover Tawwab